Forging a Great

The Brand Architecture Workshop Handbook with Worksheets

David A. Okrent

November 2017

Heart-Centric Marketing - Seattle, Washington

Forging a Great Brand
The Brand Architecture Workshop
Handbook with Worksheets
By David A. Okrent

David A. Okrent
Okrent Consulting Services
Seattle, WA 98118
info@okrentconsultingservices.com

No part of this book may be reproduced or transmitted in any form or by any means, electronic, mechanical, including photocopying, recording, or by any information storage and retrieval system, whether for commercial or non-commercial use, without written permission from the author, except for the inclusion of brief quotations in a review or scholarly work.

The purpose of this workshop guide is to educate. The author shall have no liability or responsibility to any person or entity with respect to any loss or damage caused, or alleged to have been caused, directly or indirectly, by the information and opinions contained in this workshop guide. If you do not wish to be bound by the above, please return the guide as soon as possible.

ISBN-13: 978-1979608091, ISBN-10: 1979608091, (Heart-Centric Marketing)

Copyright 2015, 2017, by David A. Okrent, all rights reserved worldwide

Everything you need to run a brand workshop

Great brands are not the result of slogans, kitschy logos, edgy advertisements, or viral videos, they are the cumulative relevant experiences of the market with the firm's people, processes, and offerings over time. This makes sense, but how do you know what experiences are needed or how these experiences are informed by the definition of the firm's brand? This is the purpose of this handbook, to provide a step-by-step process you can use to take a firm from developing a brand strategy to identifying and defining the behaviors that deliver a relevant and authentic brand to the market.

This book is for consultants, marketers, product managers, and others interested in developing a meaningful, relevant, and successful brand; where success is measured by the firm's sustainable growth. Brands are not about clicks and impressions, they are about a community of people working together to generate value for others and themselves through relationship. In this guide you may have your ideas about business and brands challenged in a way that I hope will expand your awareness and take you to a new level of practice.

Ultimately, this book is focused on helping you be successful at conducting a Brand Architecture Workshop. It starts with some general notes from the trenches and goes on to guide you from pre-work, through the workshop, and then, on to some key items for starting down the road to implementation. The process itself starts with an Environmental Assessment and moves through to a SWOT Analysis, opportunity selection, and then on to customer segmentation, the firm's traits, and finally you make a gentle turn towards the finish line with the brand promise, pillars, attributes, and the brand personality defined. The ladder sections are what guide the transformation of the firm into a brand customer want and want to promote.

This book is design for anyone, but it's written primarily for marketing and business consultants wanting to make money from helping firms build great brands. For those not as familiar with marketing, you may want to purchase my second book with the same first title. The other book provides more background on branding and has additional worksheets to help you further.

Enjoy the book. Help others be successful. Have fun.

This book is dedicated to Elizabeth - my wife and friend and my children Jacob and Sarai.

Table of Contents

Introduction 1
Level Setting 2
   Brand is a Perception 2
   The Logo and Name Are Not the Brand 2
   Brands are Behaved 3
   Pay-Off: A Strong Brand 4
   You are the Target Market for the Guide 4
   The Core is Enclosed 5
   It Takes a Group 5
   Note on Brand Revitalization 5
   Shameless Plug 5
Finches, Love, Birthdays, and Behaviors 6
About the Process 8
   Creating the Brand 8
   Brand is a Business Strategy 8
   The Top-Down Approach 9
   Process Overview 10
   House of Brands or Branded House 11
Words and Brains 12
   Words to Lose and Words to Use 12
   Get Emotional 13
   More on Words 13
   Vocabulary Disconnects 14
   Almost a Last Word on Words 14
A Few Notes from the Front Lines 16
   Before I Run a Workshop 16
   Two-Days, but… 16
   Team Facilitation 17
   Set-Up 17
   Rules of the Road 18

Where is the Agenda?	19
Everyone Needs a Break	19
Revealing the Statue	19
Mix it Up	20
Don't Take the First Answer	21
Riding Off into the Sunset	21
First, Get Commitment for Next Steps	21
Worksheets	22
Three Questions Before Acting	23
Personas	23
Give Gentle Pokes	23
Worksheet 1 – Business Environment	**25**
Business Environment	25
Side Trip Back to Houses and Brands	25
Worksheet 2 – SWOT Analysis	**29**
It's a Four-Dimensional Assessment	29
Business Objectives and Strategies	30
Worksheet 3 – Target Customer Segment	**33**
"All you need is love…"	33
I am the Same – I am Unique	34
Experience at Achievement	34
Got Linked?	35
Segmentation Analysis	35
Worksheet 4: Segment Summary	**38**
Worksheet 5 – Firm's Personality Defined	**40**
Overview	40
Values, Disconnects, and Compromises	41
Heroes and Allies	42
Raison d'Être – Reason for Being	42
Worksheet 6: DreamProspects.com	**45**
Worksheet 7 – Courtship	**47**
Worksheet 8 – Differentiation	**52**

- Differentiation Effects Margin 52
- First-Mover Differentiation 53
- The Firm's Differentiation Strategy 54
- Future History 54

Worksheet 9 – Purpose 57
- Overview 57
- Why, How, and What 57
- Purpose, Vision, and Mission 58
- Quality and Great Customer Service 58
- Purpose Statement Examples 59

Worksheet 10 – Brand Architecture 63
- A Promise Supported by Pillars 63
- Linkage 63
- Behavioral and Operational Attributes 64

Worksheet 11 - Documenting the Brand Architecture- Part 1 67

Worksheet 12 - Behavioral and Operational Attribute Narratives 69
- Example - Adventurous 70
- A Peak at Implementation 70

Worksheet 13 - Documenting the Architecture: Part 2 73

Worksheet 14 – Brand Personality 76
- A Familiar Process 76

Worksheet 15 – Positioning Statement 80
- Positioning Statement Structure: 80
- Positioning Statement Example 80

Bottoms Up: Doing the Process in Reversing 83

Wow – Impressive 84

Using the Worksheets 85

Introduction

It was a dark and stormy night when a stalwart, suave, and rugged looking man of obvious maturity and wisdom sat down in front of his computer and began to codify over a decade of his work for future generations. Full disclosure, it was a light drizzle. Perhaps not so suave and rugged, and not as altruistic as providing for future generations, but yes, documenting my "proven on the field of marketing" process for people to use today. But I would rather go with my story, I sound much more incredible in that narrative.

I started this book around 2003; although I didn't have publishing in mind at the time. It began as part of a two-week cubcation at an undisclosed corporate location; where I sat down for the first time to document the Brand Workshops I had been doing informally. Later, thanks to Dan, I found myself in the Ukraine testing the workshop with him as co-lead. From there as they say (whoever they are), the rest is history. Well my history.

This book is one of two. The other is, "Forging a Great Brand – The Comprehensive DIY Guide for Any Business," which, as the name implies, can be used alone, or it can serve as source materials for participants in the two- or three-day workshop describe in this book. The DIY book contains more background materials and each block on the summary sheet is expanded into its own worksheet. This book is written for people who already have a fair amount of knowledge in brand marketing. Interesting crazy fact, the instructor's guide was written in 2015, then the DIY book in 2017, and this is the revision to the 2015 instructor's guide. Sounds kind of backwards? It's a chicken or egg thing.

The DIY book didn't take two-years to write. I took a break after the first draft to write two other short books called "Live Stress Free – The Little Big Book of Stress Prevention," and "Build a Stress Free Team – A Guide for Leaders and Managers." True, it was a bit of a departure from branding and my other business consulting activities, but not unrelated. I have found that all business and brand issues originate from personal issues - baggage. Therefore, I spent some time getting more familiar and able to work on these issues as part of my mission to help firms grow in healthy and sustainable ways. This has moved me more into what I call "business therapy." So, take a deep breath, exhale slowly while you relax your shoulders, let go of all the distractions, and let's begin.

Level Setting

Brand is a Perception

Every company, organization, and person have a brand – a reputation and/or something someone associates with the firm or individual. Whether it's a local burger joint, a friend, and even a passing stranger they all carry a brand. It's the story, beliefs, or reputation we apply when we see, hear, or think about the person or thing. The brand is a mind-body construct pulled together from the sum of our direct and indirect experiences, feelings, cultural beliefs, values, related associations and memories, and assumptions and judgments. In other words, it's our internal image and belief about the person or thing and a projection of its future impact on ourselves. The firm's brand exists in duality; an individual belief and as a set of common beliefs shared by a group of people – the market.

During a lecture I gave on brand creation, I put up a series of three slides. The first slide contained the image of a famous male comedian and I asked the audience what they knew about this person. Then I put up a slide with a picture of a female singer and asked the same question. I then pointed out these are their individual brands. Next, I put up a slide with a picture of a stranger in a Belgium train station and asked the same question as before. People began to construct a story or brand for this person - someone they knew nothing about. We are constantly trying to make sense of our environment to better navigate through our worlds. As we make this journey we tend to consciously and unconsciously "brand" the people, places, and things coming into our senses and thoughts, that is, we judge and label. Part of this judgment is a reflection of our own self-image, fears, and motivations.

Although each person creates their own perception and meaning of a specific brand, the objective of the company or organization is to create a set of meaningful, relevant, and repeatable experiences that attempt to establish a common definition, expectation, and belief with a specific audience or market. The firm attempts to create a brand and hopes it sticks. Unfortunately, for many companies and organizations the process of creating their brand is often a mixture of unconscious and conscious intention rather than a fully conscious stepwise process – definition, planning, resourcing, and implementation.

This guide provides a detailed systematic workshop process for defining the brand and for identifying the essential components needed to deliver one that is highly relevant and valued. Combined with its sister book, it's the most comprehensive brand architecture development process ever put to print (in my opinion). The early parts of this process are applicable to strategic planning and product development.

The Logo and Name Are Not the Brand

Many companies focus their brand development solely on creating a catchy name and logo. However, the choice of a name or graphic is not important; these are only symbols for the brand, they are not the brand. The name and logo serve as memory cues to help the potential customer recall what they know about the firm and its offerings. One goal of this process is to identify what will resonant with the target market first and then, to use this information to inform the choice of the firm's name and design of its logo.

As the instructor you will be fighting upstream with firms that get fixated on creating the perfect logo before anything else. Don't fight, let them come up with that first, if they insist. In the end, the results of the workshop and the follow-on work to make the brand real will give meaning to the name and logo.

Brands are Behaved

Over a decade ago, I began focusing on brand development and management. During the early years of this work I spent time learning, thinking, and experimenting on what creates a strong brand - one that would garner the highest value in the market.

Generally, the brand can be defined as the market's total collective impressions of the firm and its offerings through direct and indirect knowledge and experiences. However, that doesn't explain how to create a brand, let alone a great one. Thus, my focus fell on how a firm can consciously create a fantastic brand. FANtastic – a brand that people identify with, contribute to, and promote.

What I eventually determined, and confirmed, is brands are the outcomes of behaviors; simply, "brands are behaved." A firm must behave its way into the hearts and minds of its target market based on what is meaningful to the customer while being differentiated from its competitors. Frankly, advertising doesn't create the brand, experience does. Great firms define and behave their brand first, and after they've deliver on it consistently begin using advertising to set an expectation and build awareness with a wider audience. Again, the brand is created by the firm's behaviors through its people, processes, and offerings. This is what gives meaning to the name and logo.

Companies with strong identities generally have significantly integrated their unique brand behaviors into their organization and offerings. This can be by plan or chance. One of the jobs of Promotional Marketing and Communications (Public Relations) is to establish an expectation in the market of the benefits and experiences the customers will have with the firm. When customers consistently experience the fulfillment of these expectations a positive brand is born and a preference for the firm over its competitors develops. If the firm's behaviors are not congruent with the expectations, then the firm develops an inferior brand and a short lifespan. This is a good reason for establishing the firm's behaviors and ability to deliver on them consistently in a subsection of the market before setting expectations broadly.

> *A brand is the result of the knowledge and experiences the market has with the firm directly or indirectly through its people, processes, offerings, and promotions. Potential customers can indirectly gain knowledge, imagine experiences, and draw conclusions based on the opinions of others. For example, via Yelp and Amazon.com reviews.*

When I was a teenager I worked for a market research firm. It was a long time ago, during the ancient dark times before the Internet, cell phones, and craft beers. I was part of a team gathering information on the brand strength and preference for a specific beer. The recurring message I heard from hundreds of people was clear, "We love the ads and hate the beer." (People in the Seattle-area here's a hint, beer bottles running near a mountain road.) If you only measured brand by advertising recall or buzz the firm would have been rated as a strong brand, but ads were not their product. The beer wasn't selling well compared to their competitors. Buzz is irrelevant, if the customers don't buy. Beware the advertising firm that doesn't measure results by sales impact. Total impressions should translate to increased sales. However, in long sales cycle times, like two or more years, the ratio of impression to conversion to qualified lead may be the only hint of the connection to a future sale.

The market's perceptions determine if the firm's brand is labeled strong, neutral, or weak. The firm has no authority to anoint itself a "great brand." It's like "coolness," if the person states they are cool they aren't; because cool people don't announce they're cool. The crowd bestows the label. Great brands know when they achieved greatness by experiencing consistently good or fantastic sales over their competition. Lots of social media posts can be a nice indicator, but they don't pay the bills.

Figuring out what these brand behaviors are and how to integrate them into the company or product led me to create the Brand Workshop Series. Over the course of a decade, these workshops have been refined based on the implementation of their results. There are five workshops in the series each one consisting of two or three-days of intensive work. This book supports the first in the series, the *Brand Architecture Workshop.*

Pay-Off: A Strong Brand

The goal of the workshop process is to provide a firm with a blueprint for creating a strong memorable brand. If the firm is committed to converting the blueprint into reality it will reap benefits like a loyal customer base, easier access to capital, support for a higher offering price, attention by trade and other media, and higher employee retention and productivity rates. This assumes the firm implements the findings. Follow through for more than a year is always difficult in the corporate setting.

You are the Target Market for the Guide

This workbook and guide is for business consultants, marketers, brand managers, product managers, owners, CEOs, CMOs, entrepreneurs, and anyone that wants to improve the success rate of their business endeavors. The information and worksheets in this guide will help build a fantastic brand.

The guide portion of this book is not a comprehensive textbook on brand development and management. It's my notes and thoughts on the workshop, some commentary on branding, and a little preaching from the pulpit thrown in. I provide some background to support each worksheet and some commentary on how to use them. Profits and non-profit organizations will find this guide and its worksheets equally helpful on defining their brands. More detail can be found in the other book of the same first title already mentioned.

The Core is Enclosed

Missing from this document are the exercises, participant training materials (for example, what is a brand and why it affects the bottom line), and other worksheets that provide input to the ones enclosed. These are omitted because I find each instructor likes to develop their own versions of these items. However, you will find more detail materials in the DIY version of this book.

In each block on the worksheets there are sufficient questions to help guide the user in completing the sheet. Many of these blocks or questions may be broken out as separate worksheets and exercises if desired. There is a description section before each worksheet where I touch on some of the additional activities I use during a workshop. Of course, these sheets don't provide the answer; they are only a vehicle to help arrive at the definition of the company's or organization's brand.

It Takes a Group

It's best to do the worksheets in a group consisting of different levels of management, members of all departments, key non-managers, and people of different ages and backgrounds. Keep the numbers to less than twenty-five. In cases where the firm is a start-up or relatively small it is still best to do the work in a group; bring in friends and others to help.

Note on Brand Revitalization

Before starting a brand revitalization program first solve the business issue that triggered the need; otherwise the outcome will be less than ideal. To put it bluntly, stop the bleeding, find the root cause of the problem, and fix it. The process of fixing the problem begins the process of restoring faith in the company and revitalizing the brand. I would estimate brand revitalization taking two-years.

Shameless Plug

Here is a list of some of the workshops I offer:

Workshop 1 – Brand Architecture

Workshop 2 – The Brand Implementation Plan

Workshop 3 – Brand Personality and Expression

Workshop 4 – Managing for Brand

Workshop 5 – Customer Loyalty by Design

Strategic Planning Seminar

Integrated MARCOM Planning Workshop

Business Therapy Weekend Intensive

Finches, Love, Birthdays, and Behaviors

After almost a decade of doing work in brand development, creating workshops, and delivering lectures it occurred to me one day that everything could be summed in four key terms: Finches, Love, Birthdays, and Behaviors. Honestly, it occurred when I was sharing my materials to help prepare Anthony for a presentation. Shortly after having this insight I was asked to give a lecture on brand development at the Product Management Consortium – test market. I decided to throw out my standard lecture and create one based on these four items. Well the presentation went well and to this day the people who attended remember the formula through the title "Finches, Love, Birthdays, and Behaviors – The Four Keys to a Great Brand."

What does this mean? Finches refers to "Darwin's Finches," which is about differentiation – a key to competitiveness and an item the brand should evoke. Love is about forming an unconditional relationship with the target market that is mutually beneficial to both and not exploitive of either. Birthdays refers to gifts, that is, products or services that are meaningful to the customer because the firm knows its customers' (partner's) likes, dislikes, needs wants, and aspirations. The last key is behaviors. These are the nuts and bolts of how a brand is created and delivered. How many marriages are strengthened or broken by the behaviors of the involved individuals? The same is true of relations between the firm and the market.

As a firm goes through this process those involved should keep these four items in mind. You will find I dip in and out of the dating and marriage analogy throughout the book. This is related to the language of the four keys. There are two other items to keep in mind during this process: amnesia and stronger/weaker.

In 2007, I gave a talk at a market research conference in Amsterdam regarding measuring and improving customer satisfaction and loyalty. This was a conference of about three hundred researchers representing the more analytical side of Marketing. I tend to practice across the entire Marketing continuum from highly analytical and processed based to fuzzy and artistic, but I digress.

I was the third speech of the day. The first two speeches were highly technical, data-driven, and very dry presentations that although interesting were presented so flat the audience had fallen asleep. When I got up on stage and looked out it appeared to me that most of the group was checked out or snoring. I needed to get the energy up in the room.

To my surprise the next thing I did was yelled out, "*AMNESIA*." This startled the audience awake. Now all their attention was on me, unfortunately I didn't know why I yelled amnesia. To buy myself time to think I yelled it again – "*AMNESIA*." Then it came to me. The next thing I said was, "Why, when we walk into our offices do we get amnesia? We seem to forget what it's like to be a customer. We absentmindedly go about creating customer policies and practices we would not want to experience ourselves?" Then I transition to my material on measuring customer loyalty.

Is the firm asleep? Is the firm suffering from amnesia? If you answered yes to either one; fix it or help them fix it; otherwise they won't be able to create an optimal brand. When going through this process fight amnesia. Great brands put themselves in their customers' shoes to ensure the firm "does unto others what they want done to them" while making a fair, healthy, and sustainable profit.

The last item is stronger/weaker. It's the one question that can guide the entire firm in every moment once the brand is defined. Here's the question, "Is what I am about to do going to make the brand stronger or weaker?" It's possible the best answer may be "weaker." Take a moment and consider when weaker might be the best answer.

I was once asked to support a department fighting against having a percentage of their customer support budget cut by their executive team (CEO, COO, etc.). Cost cutting was in full swing. When the time came, I was asked what the potential impact the proposed cut would have on the strength of the brand and the level of customer loyalty. Of course, I said it would be adversely impacted, but the budget was cut anyway. The result wasn't a surprise to me. After this decision, my advice to the Customer Support group was to aggressively manage their operations and relationships to minimize the reduction in loyalty and loss of brand strength. Many groups understand how to increase loyalty, but they may not know how to consciously mitigate situations that will cause it to drop.

Another theme of this book and process is…

Conscious brand management

About the Process

Creating the Brand

The brand is the result of the beliefs and behaviors of the firm as expressed through its people, processes, offerings, and promotions. Therefore, to create a strong brand the firm should pick the right behaviors and express them via their workforce, processes, and offerings. But how does the firm know what are these right behaviors? Well there are two methods for finding these key behaviors. The first method is to select the behaviors or key items one wants, define them in detail, and then build the company around them.

Building the company around the brand consists of actions like training people on how to deliver the brand, developing processes and design guidelines to support the brand, learning to manage and hire for brand, and creating offerings to express the brand. The other method is a strategic top-down process for discovering the behavioral elements that attract and retain a specific set of customers. Once the behaviors are known the building process moves forward as noted above.

I don't think the former method is as effective at maximizing success as following the top-down method this book presents. The top-down method generally eliminates many of the bumps and eddies the firm may experience using the other approach. However, the elegance of my process is the firm can run it in reverse. They can select the firm's attributes at the start and then work this guide from the back to the front. This means going from behaviors to figuring out what market segment is best served by those behaviors, then identifying what the segment wants, and finally selecting the opportunity that will enable the firm to profit. If the firm wants to go back-to-front, please read the book forward first then focus on the chapter, "Bottoms Up."

People involved in software development may find this process a bit too structured, they may even label it "waterfall." Hey, waterfall is not a dirty word. However, this is more like Agile, we are starting first by creating the business requirements and then as we progress you will begin to recognize things that fit epics, features, and stories. Lastly, brand management is a never-ending feedback process between the firm and market leading to continuous refinement.

Brand is a Business Strategy

The thesis "brands are behaved," may need a little more clarification. The brand is an expression of a business strategy and market position that supports a business objective. Achieving the brand strategy occurs through organizational structures, training, and by implementing a set of operational, design, pricing, marketing, communications, and other imperatives. These are all defined or informed by the brand architecture.

The Top-Down Approach

The goal of the process is to establish a brand that lives at the three-way intersection (insert mental Venn Diagram here) of the firm's personality and capabilities, the customers' aspirations and needs, and a defensible competitive position. I also emphasize building and implementing a brand that fosters a long-term loving relationship with the customer base. The market loves fantastic brands and fantastic brands love their customers, potential customers, and non-customers alike. More on love later.

My method starts with understanding the business environment, then moves to developing the brand strategy and architecture, and finally to identifying behaviors and tactics for delivering the brand. This flow may be a bit more work upfront, but I think it results in a better foundation for success. There is some redundancy in the process, where variations of a few questions reappear on a few worksheets. These redundancies are opportunities to re-evaluate and refine materials based on how the information is evolving in the process. At times, this may trigger a need to pivot the business.

There are twelve steps in the process:

1. Business Environmental Assessment
2. SWOT Analysis
3. Identifying the Target Customer Segment
4. Determining the Firm's Personality
5. Creating a Profile for the Firm
6. Identifying Commonality with the Segment
7. Differentiation
8. Purpose, Mission, and Vision
9. Brand Promise
10. Brand Attributes
11. Brand Personality
12. Positioning Statement

It may be surprising that it takes eight steps to get to the brand definition. However, until the basic information of what the firm wants to achieve in the world, what type of customers it wants, what are the potential customers' desires, and how it will stand out among crowd are known, the brand can't be well defined. With this information, the firm can design a brand that aligns with a customer segment in a meaningful way.

There will be a tendency to skip steps under the assumption "we already know this about our firm or offering." However, as the consultant, take the time to question what is assumed, poke at those sacred beliefs and find out what's true. Here is a great way to test "we all know this." If a group is starting the process together or you are briefing executives at a pre-workshop meeting, have everyone write down what they believe is the purpose of the firm. Then have a few people read them aloud to the group. How much variation was there from person-to-person? Maybe the group isn't on the same page. A fundamental rule of life; check assumptions before acting.

Process Overview

It begins with a Business Environmental Assessment followed by a SWOT Analysis and then the selection of an opportunity to pursue. It's beyond the scope of this workbook to inform the reader on how to do an environmental assessment or SWOT analysis, but there are many resources available on the Internet. The worksheets hold a summation of these items. These sheets also serve as the basis for a strategic planning process.

Can these two sections be skipped? Yes, if they already have the information. If this hasn't been done I would suggest helping them do it. At the least, if they have it undocumented the act of writing it down will help get the group to the same level of understanding.

Often the firm has a preconceived idea of what offering it will apply to a segment before doing an environmental assessment and SWOT analysis. However, having this bias isn't optimal and it usually isn't a good idea if the firm is going after a new market or adjacency. Once an opportunity is found, evaluated, and selected the firm can decide to build a specific brand for the new item (house of brands) or not (branded house).

Next a customer type or segment is identified having the highest motivation for the selected opportunity. Part of this process is examining the common characteristics of the customers in the segment based on psychosocial, aspirational, physical, regulatory, emotional, and economic factors. After this is done, an assessment of the firm's personality is made to determine where it intersects with the segment. Ideally, there should be some intersection between the customers' and the firm's values, beliefs, and/or interests. We tend to be more inclined to those that are most like us.

If the firm is just starting up, already exists and desires to improve its relevance to the target segment, or needs to revitalize its brand this is the point where the new personality begins to be defined. At this juncture, a general description of what the firm can provide that is relevant and meaningful to the segment usually becomes clear. However, the exact specifications for an offering cannot be fully defined yet – that's another process. Armed with this information the firm can create its big idea and competitive differentiation strategy.

Now, it gets more brand-like. From here the company can formulate its purpose, vision, mission, and brand promise. The brand promise comes from restating the company's purpose or point of differentiation from the point of view of the target segment. Developing the brand architecture occurs after the brand promise.

The promise sits on three to five supporting pillars. These pillars are the strategies enabling the realization of the brand promise. Each pillar has an additional eight to ten behaviors and/or operational attributes that support them. The behaviors and attributes are what make the pillars possible. Think of the pillars as strategic and the behaviors and operational attributes as tactics.

Once the behaviors and attributes are determined, they each receive a descriptive narrative to illustrate how they come together. The narratives guide the internal development of the brand. This becomes more understandable later in the guide.

Next comes a positioning statement. This statement has many of the elements of a value proposition or elevator speech; however, its primary purpose is to help guide the Marketing and Communications Team in developing the promotional plan. Finally, the brand personality is codified using items like color, music, textures, and themes. The firm can address the design of the logo and name of the firm or offering at this point.

House of Brands or Branded House

The process helps develop a firm's, a product's, or a service's brand; however, first determine if the firm is a "house of brands," or a "branded house." In a house of brands each offering has its own brand identity and presence in the market. Proctor and Gamble, for example, has thousands of products and each has its own brand identity; they are a house of brands. In a branded house, offerings support the parent company's name and brand. Black and Decker has many products too, but they all carry the parent company name; they are a branded house. There are also companies, like Microsoft, that use a mixture of both. There will be more on this later.

Words and Brains

Words to Lose and Words to Use

"Hundreds of butterflies flitted in and out of sight like short-lived punctuation marks in a stream of consciousness without beginning or end." - Haruki Murakami.

Business Version: "I saw a lot of butterflies today. "

Language impacts us in many overt and subtle ways. It can expand our thinking or contract it like a punctured balloon. Sometimes it can empower and rally to action; other times it can arrive tired, worn out, or stillborn. It can sound like the harmony of an orchestra or a staccato of a politician's measured and stilted words. It can be full of jargon or light, lyrical and full of life. Words matter, and the most memorable phrases are ones that touch us on many different levels: visual, auditory, emotional, physical, spiritual, etc.

When I conduct workshops, I introduce people to the simple three-brain model; reptilian, limbic, and cognitive. This is a bit overly simplistic, but it does the job. The reptilian brain, the oldest, is focused on survival: eating, breathing, fleeing, protecting, reproducing, etc. When politicians and many non-profits put out messages emphasizing real or potential threats to children they are appealing to this part of the brain. If the reptilian is activated successfully it will over-ride the limbic and cognitive processes. Therefore, a logical rebuttal rarely changes minds when used against reptilian messages.

The limbic system is focused on our emotions, emotional needs, and our unconscious beliefs and drivers. When the reptilian isn't activated, this part of the brain is where most decisions are made. When both are activated, look out. The take away here is simple, decisions are almost never made by the cognitive parts of the brain. The cognitive areas are great with facts and data and do well to help justify a decision, but generally, this section isn't making the decision. In fact, the cognitive brain will do its best to create a story, to put all the pieces (external stimuli and internal processing) together in a way that will appear to make sense, even if it doesn't.

This means we appeal to either the reptilian or the limbic first using emotional, dynamic, and illustrative words to carry our messages; we speak to potential customers' motivations and/or drivers. Then we provide facts and data to help their cognitive brains support closing the deal they have already agreed to act on. Also, illustrative language and stories help secure the firm's messages into the customers' long-term memory. However, there must be a truth in this to work; otherwise, you will leave the person with a bitter after-taste that may reduce brand strength.

Brand is conveyed by repeatable customer-relevant experiences and through powerful language that ties the customers' motivations, aspirations, and drives to the firm and/or its offerings. We are not excluding images, sound, textures, or video at all. But everything starts with the words. Many people get worried that we are saying that every message or brochure needs to be a novel. This isn't the case; we are looking for an economy of powerful words, analogies, and metaphors as well as imagery and sound. Our goal is tight motivational and memorable communication. A story helps to convey the emotion and outcome as well as create a framework for forming memory and later recall.

Get Emotional

Throughout these worksheets, you will need to remind the participants to eliminate corporate or technical speak and to focus on language that triggers a multi-sensory experience in the minds of the target market. Language that is emotive, dynamic, and illustrative helps create long-term memories.

Several years ago, I was working with members of an opera company who wanted to increase their membership; I asked them each to tell me their "elevator pitch." Within a few words, I started hearing the usual corporate buzzwords like "premier and world-class." In fact, it sounded so corporate that I could have replaced the name of the opera company with a chemical firm and it would have still sounded true, well close to true.

After hearing these sterile arias, I asked them to tell me about the time they first fell in love with opera. As you can imagine, I heard some very emotional and vivid words and phrases. I asked them, "Why wasn't this beautiful language part of their elevator pitches?" Their response at first was silence and then the light bulbs started glowing over their heads from dull red to bright orange and soon to an intense radiating white light. They got it, sharing from the heart is how we really communicate. Remember when helping them complete the worksheets encourage them to use language that is dynamic and emotive, even if the question doesn't explicit ask. The more you can build trust with the attendees and create a safe space the greater the chance they will take risks and be more vulnerable.

More on Words

Corporate-speak and jargon are the words we think we need to use to sound educated and to show we are part of the business or technical club. These are the over used cognitive words of the MBA school, engineer, scientist, pilot, or other discipline. It's all jargon. Jargon is often touted as shorthand to make communications more efficient and this may be true, but it's also true that it denotes a division between those in the club - those having secret knowledge, and everyone else. Them or us, is not a healthy situation for communication. Also, by using corporate speak, abbreviations, and jargon the message and meaning conveyed are often lost or limited.

The letters PARS stand for Pain-Anxiety Reduction System. Now that you know what PARS stands for how do you process the next two sentences? "Our PARS improves patient comfort and lowers anxiety by 30% over traditional dosing." "Our Pain-Anxiety Reduction System improves patient comfort and lowers anxiety by 30% over traditional dosing." When you read PARS did you mentally hear or see the words or just read the letters? Generally, you only saw the letters or the sound "pars;" therefore, the emotional or aspirational meaning and triggers the words would have created are lost. But I can't keep writing the full term out every time. Why not? It's just words on a page. Are there places where an abbreviation does work? Yes, there are no absolutes here. For example, one might use abbreviations to exploit, manipulate those seeking to maintain club exclusivity. However, is that an expression of love?

Corporate-speak is just silly cognitive crap that communicates little. For example, what the heck does world-class mean? What defines it? Who awards the title? How do you know when you attain it? If the firm already does global business, isn't the firm world-class by default? Meaningless corporate-speak. These and jargon will become the "Forbidden Words," or words to lose during the workshop. I will come back to this subject later.

When these words are removed from the firm some people may get a bit uncomfortable. This is normal. They are initially confused or stressed because they may no longer know how to talk about the firm or its offerings. However, they will recover and discover a much more powerful vocabulary. Two things I tell attendees: 1) express ideas using language that a twelve-year old would understand and 2) express your positive passion in the workshop as you would outside of work.

But we are engineers, we don't use this emotive, highly illustrative language. We are objective and rational. Trust me, I have proven to many engineers they are not objective, but that's a different essay. I have a technical background, so these types of statements don't register with me. Many engineers and technical types say this, but it's their corporate or guild persona speaking. When they speak to each other their language is anything but dry and emotionless. Ever come up with a beautifully elegant design or solution?

Vocabulary Disconnects

During the workshop it's a good practice to get people to define key strategic terms as they use them. Often, we assume everyone has the same meaning as we do, but this isn't a good assumption. It's a good practice to formally define the firm's key or strategic words or terms to ensure understanding.

I call definitions that don't align across the enterprise "strategic vocabulary disconnects." Strategic vocabularies are terms used to communicate the direction and actions of the firm. For example, when a leader says, "We are going to increase our rate of *innovation*" there is often an assumption that everyone has the same meaning for the term innovation; however, until this assumption is confirmed you don't know. For example, what if the people who are charged with making the firm more innovative don't have the same definition as the leader? Do you think this will cause any issues? Not having the same meaning to key terms can lead to misunderstanding, frustration, tension, and failure without any awareness by the parties as to why things didn't work. Vocabulary disconnects are like two people building a tunnel from opposite ends who don't realize they use the same words – meter, foot, or degree but have each assigned a different standard of measure to them. One may define a degree as being sixty seconds and the other uses forty-eight; oops.

As you conduct the workshop probe on the meaning of key terms. Check with the participants if they all have the same meaning or not. This helps get people into agreement, eventually.

Almost a Last Word on Words

Often, I will get words like happy, satisfied, etc. over and over again as I ask people to list outcomes and desires for the firm and/or the customer. At this point I will often select two or three people to volunteer for a little probing, one at a time. Generally, it is a few rounds of, "What makes you [feeling]?" They answer. "What does that provide you?" They answer. "How does that feel?" They answer, and we continue this process about three times. This generally creates more meaningful words. However, be careful if you use this process, you may drop into one of their subconscious issues. If you sense this going to happen or you brush up against it - stop immediately, thank them and move on.

A Few Notes from the Front Lines

Before I Run a Workshop

Before running a workshop, I sit down with the requesting group's upper management or CEO to find out what the business situation is and what their objectives are. What triggered the need? Next, I interview key people and/or the management team one-on-one to get a more comprehensive view and a better sense of the corporate culture. I will sometimes also interview key accounts or customers to get an outside perspective. More formal research maybe needed to get a deeper sense of how the firm is perceived externally.

Next, I survey the potential participants in the workshop and other key employees to get more information on employee and management perceptions of the firm, the brand, and competitors. It is important to get the workforce's perception on what they think the market believes about the brand and their competitors, as what they believe is generally telegraphed consciously and/or subconsciously to the world.

Within my workforce survey are two open-ended questions to get at the language they use to express the firm and its brand. I farm these questions and their company manifestos for corporate-speak. In the workshop these terms and those like them will become *forbidden words* (mentioned in the previous section). I do this to help participants move towards finding more active, dynamic, and emotional words to express the firm and its brand. The goal is to get a new, more powerful vocabulary to better communicate the brand. I am a bit more relaxed on the forbidden words at the start of the workshop and tighten up on it as I progress. Some people experience less shock this way.

Prior to the workshop, inform all participants not to schedule meetings or calls during the workshop period. Also, tell them they may not use cell phones and computers during sessions. It's best not to surprise people regarding these items on the morning of the workshop. Emergencies of course are the exception. If people can't comply they are excused, if the workshop falls below a quorum then it should be rescheduled. One more thing, there are no observers, everyone participates.

Two-Days, but...

Ideally, workshops should run for two-days and in some cases three-days, but the ideal is not often available or supported. If the workshop duration is less than two-days, some pieces get completed outside of the original workshop. Less than two-days will add more reviews and refinement time to the final report as it goes back around multiple times for input and comments from attendees. Full agreement by everyone on every item rarely happens, at some point a leader must decide or the results just end up weakened to please everyone. If it's one-day or less, then they may not be ready to commit to improving their brand. This can be done in half-day sessions, but you will need to add a fifth half-day to compensate for review and getting back on track.

Team Facilitation

Generally, I do my workshops with an additional facilitator. Team facilitation has proven to be very effective. The lead facilitator is the one who initiates the project. This person has project responsibility and oversees customizing and managing the workshop. The second facilitator comes in anytime from the interview stage to just a few days before the session.

The second facilitator assists with the sessions and helps create the post-seminar report. They share the workload during the workshop and while one is facilitating the other is monitoring the participants' engagement level. During breaks or while the small teams are working they check-in with each other to make adjustments, if needed. Facilitators should be skilled in team teaching and facilitation, interpersonal communication, rapport building, and knowledgeable of business practices and structures. Team-facilitation requires both people to spend considerable time before a workshop to work out chorography and to build trust between each other. If the facilitators are not aligned in the workshop, it may feel to the attendees that mom and dad are fighting. Not a good situation.

If one of the facilitators believes the workshop agenda needs adjusting, for example, due to time or an unexpected surprise, they call an unscheduled break. This gives the facilitators time to discuss, agree, plan, and prepare the materials. If it's a very significant change, they will discuss it with the workshop sponsors and then the attendees; otherwise, they don't mention it.

Significant changes sometimes occur when an issue that can affect the foundation of the business is uncovered. These issues are often not surprises, but have been ignored or denied by the management team. Often these issues are uncovered during the preliminary work. Diplomacy is important in these situations, especially when these issues surface at the workshop. This process is not about blame, but on learning and moving forward.

I ran one workshop where the head of the program and the head of sales were slightly at odds with each other. The sales person was not being direct, but was always poking at whatever the program leader said. Finally, I ask the sales person what was going on. He told me and the group they were not aligned with the market's timeline. At that point I called a break and altered my course. When they came back, I worked with the group to go through the market timeline with respect to their business operation; an hour deviation. Turned out they were one-year late to market with a five-year opportunity window. Sales was living it and the rest were in denial. From here forward we focused the workshop on how to get into a better market position. Finishing the brand came later, we had to ensure there was going to be a business that needed a brand. This doesn't often happen, but it can.

Set-Up

My preference is to use round tables with only half of the table having chairs and those chairs facing front. If only rectangular tables are available, I set them up in a chevron design and slightly offset so everyone can see the front. I put one or two rectangular tables to the back of the room for the facilitators to use. Each participant's table has sticky notes, masking tape, pens, and blank paper available as well as a flip chart and easel nearby. I like the flip charts with the sticky upper backs.

A digital projector, screen, and a computer for showing the worksheets and other presentation materials are a necessity. I also, highly recommend using a remote radio frequency or infrared trigger for navigating through the presentation slides. These aren't expensive and provide an added degree of freedom. Try not to use the projector and computer at one of the participant tables; it's less disruptive to the attendees if a separate small table or stand is used.

Early in the workshop the group will be divided into small teams. I don't let people pick their teams, we count off in threes, fours, or fives to create three to five randomly selected teams. Sometimes I will need to balance the teams by individual function even after randomization. I rotate the leadership of the team as much as possible. Don't push people who are indicating they don't want to lead. Be aware that mixing people of different ranks on the same team may not work well in some cultures.

Rules of the Road

After welcoming comments, introductions, and safety information I establish and get agreement on the rules below. Modify these as needed to fit the audience.

- No use of cell phones or computers by attendees during the actual sessions
- Do not schedule meetings during the session times
- Everyone is of equal rank, except the facilitators
- The facilitator will not reveal the detail agenda, any exercises, or worksheets before they are needed
- Discussion is encouraged; however, the facilitators may stop an exchange and record the item on the "For Future Discussion" list
- Respect each other and treat each other with courtesy
- Each of us is 100% responsible for our actions and reactions
- No one can make you feel or think anything, see rule above
- Anyone can call a "Time Out," for a physical or psychological safety reason
- Do not make assumptions; ask questions and seek clarity
- If you need something, ask; you may get it
- If you are uncomfortable with anything make it known to the facilitators
- All discussions in the workshop stay in the workshop
- Try to listen without constructing a reply
- Only give feedback when asked. Don't offer feedback unless you first ask if it's wanted. It's okay to say "no" when asked to hear feedback. The only answer to feedback is "thank you."
- If things get heated or people get triggered it is time for a break

- The facilitators will question and challenge individuals, teams, and the group - it's not personal
- There are no bystanders in the workshop
- We suggest you let go and trust the process.

Where is the Agenda?

As you may have determined, I don't show a high-level or detailed agenda. In fact, I don't show our materials or any agenda to a client ever. It's part of my rules of engagement. There are two reasons for this: 1) the workshop is a discovery process and knowing what is coming constrains creativity, and 2) as was mentioned before, we may change the workshop as needed to adjust for the little surprises that bubble up. If the audience knows our detailed agenda, then we would have to stop, explain ourselves, and sometimes take up valuable time trying to convince people to accept the change. I do put up a purpose, process, and payoff slide after introductions.

Everyone Needs a Break

Breaks are about resting and recharging. I like people to have the freedom to get up and leave the room for a *short* break anytime they need. However, I inform the attendees not to return and then ask for a recap of what they missed. This is disruptive and slows down the process. They should wait until the next scheduled break to get caught up.

In addition to individual breaks, make sure to take group breaks periodically of no less than fifteen minutes. Lunch breaks should be an hour and are not working sessions. People need time to decompress and rest. Also, be mindful to watch for saturation in the group or a team and if it occurs either change to another activity or call a break - even if not scheduled.

When returning from scheduled breaks, or lunch, take a minute to bring everyone mentally into the room. It can be as simple as everyone taking a deep breath or through a short piece of music. Have paper on a wall where people can write jokes, sayings, or draw graffiti during breaks. The facilitators should refer to one or two of these graffiti items from time-to-time. It can help people vent or express themselves when they don't feel comfortable talking. Facilitators may need to use this graffiti board first to break the ice for the attendees.

Revealing the Statue

"Every block of stone has a statue inside it and it is the task of the sculptor to discover it."
-Michelangelo

Every workshop has the answers in it. Our task as workshop leaders is to help the participants chip away and remove the excess rock to reveal the essence inside. This is not an easy task and it takes time for participants to feel safe opening up and contributing within the process and with each other.

This is especially important if senior staff is present and in some cultures, it may not be possible to mix senior staff with non-managers.

The facilitator's job at the start is to create a "safe container" for the attendees and to provide opportunities for them to gain confidence in moving through this undiscovered country. When they feel safe and confident they can move beyond obvious or easy responses to get to the gold nuggets below. Building a safe container starts with the rules listed earlier and includes:

- Establish rapport with the group
- Communicate in a non-judgmental or non-punitive way
- Ensuring everyone has an opportunity to be heard
- Support an atmosphere of mutual trust and respect
- Help people feel and experience being empowered

In the Brand Architecture Workshop, my intent is to educate through questioning and discovery, to push beyond the obvious and to arrive at a new, more competitive concept that drives the definition of the business and the brand. After the workshop the rough sculpture gets polished before being unveiled to the firm.

At the end of the workshop there is a lot of information to be sifted through and polished. It can take up to eight days to pull all the information together into a draft document. Once the draft is complete, the facilitators meet with a small team from the client to do some additional polishing and then review it with the rest of the attendees and later upper management.

There may be a time as the facilitation team, the consultants, build the report they may discover an alternative result. When this occurs, they should write both up in the report. Often in my pre-workshop research I find a potential solution. When this happen, I record it and then I stay conscious on not influencing or polluting the workshop experience and outcome. However, the possible solution can help frame some stimulating workshop questions.

Mix it Up

Don't use just one type of exercise or way to complete the worksheets. Mix it up, use a combination of individual, small team, and whole room activities to get the best result. Provide exercises that let people express themselves using pictures instead of words. Sometimes I have them do a collage or encourage them to draw pictures of the new opportunity, future state, or the brand pillars. However, remember some people will be uncomfortable with drawing so allow them to use words. The bottom line is to vary the activities, be flexible, and help people stay out of guilt or shame if they are having trouble with an activity or way of expressing.

Don't Take the First Answer

Customer segmentation and differentiation in this guide are on one sheet; however, I generally run them as separate one-hour exercises. Other people like them as one sheet. Again, be flexible, if you want to run a section of the worksheet as a separate exercise then try it.

Here is one of the ways I facilitate customer segmentation:

> I will break the group into teams of three to five people and have each team use a flip chart easel and paper to write down how they would segment the market. After 15 minutes, I check in with each group separately to see what they came up with and I ask them to explain the reasons behind the segmentation they created. It's important to keep them focused on being concise.
>
> After hearing how they segmented the market, I remove the flip chart paper and place it to the side, and ask them to start again and try to find a different way to segment the market. I may have them repeat this up to four times. Why repeat the exercise? Because the first two or three are generally obvious, easy, typical, and often the same segments the competitors use. The last one or two attempts often exposes a new paradigm that may yield a more competitive position. Be careful to avoid frustrating and shutting down the participants.

Lastly, I test key areas such as purpose, mission, and differentiation by having them put their competitors' names in front of the statements. If they still read true then I ask them to start again until we find a unique position or strategy or until they decide, what they have is right for them. I call this the Jeff Robinson test. Hi Jeff. Jeff, one of my long-time co-facilitators, first used this method in our work together.

Riding Off into the Sunset

Before I close the workshop, I review what the group achieved, what the next steps are, who has further actions, and I go over the items on the "For Future Discussion" list (see workshop rules). After answering any questions, I then do a formal closing process that includes restating the "discussions in the workshop are confidential" and we then set the date for the review of the draft final report.

First, Get Commitment for Next Steps

Okay, they have the final report; now what? This is one of the make or break moments, because either they keep the momentum and take the next step, or they stop. Therefore, it's important to get commitment before the workshop that the firm will start a planning exercise to map out the next 24 months on the heels of the final report. The planning needs to be realistic and factor in what is achievable given the resources and time available.

Focus on developing a balanced plan, where some quick gains can be made while longer term items are underway. Getting change in motion with some quick victories helps build momentum. I suggest focusing during the first phase of implementation on product design, brand marketing, quality, service, and training managers and those that directly touch the customers.

Managers are the most important group in this process; their commitment determines whether the brand will be implemented successfully or not. Management training focuses on how to manage and hire for brand. Why be so aggressive on training managers? Because, management makes the rules, they are the priests of the corporate culture.

I highly suggest forming a cross-functional brand team led by Marketing. This team will become the group that will guide the implementation of the brand and provide mentoring to managers and others. Also, while the top-down work is forming, get started on a bottom up effort as well.

The bottom up effort starts after managers are trained. Give them sixty-days to work with their teams to select one item and only one item that they can improve with respect to brand. It must be within their immediate control, can be implemented within six months, and measurable. Recognize and celebrate each completion.

Some teams involved in the "select one item to improve" exercise may find it hard to conceptualize. For these groups it may help if they consider the people that provide them input as vendors and teams they hand-off their output to as customers. The group can then decide on an item based on getting a better input from their vendors or to help their customer (downstream) be more successful. By expressing needs, adaptability, and love upstream and downstream, the internal group can improve the delivery of the external brand.

Worksheets

The blank worksheets shown in this book and the detailed sheets that are in the DIY book are available on request via info@okrentconsultingservices.com. They are free to purchasers of either book and come in pdf and PowerPoint formats. When sending email tell me what the last word of the first paragraph on page 65 is, this is how I know you have the book. Please see worksheet use rules at the end of the book.

The worksheet numbers and block numbers on each sheet make referencing items between sheets easier. In Planning Workshops, we utilize the numbers to create a work breakdown structure for use in developing road maps and project plans. Lastly, the questions in each block are not exhaustive. They are only there to stimulate thinking.

Three Questions Before Acting

Educate the group on asking themselves these two questions during their workday:

Is what I am about to do going to strengthen or weaken the brand?

Am I making a conscious choice?

Do I need help or support to do this activity?

Personas

The first half of this process is building up a broad image or persona of three characters: the firm, the customer, and the competition. Then we take these personas and use them to help define the brand and potentially the offering. Think back to the first page when I mentioned the pictures of the comedian and the singer. Obviously, they have talent – their core competency. Next, they may have decided to strategically focus their talent to meet the needs and style of a specific customer segment. Then they may have created a public persona to fit that market niche – a brand. This is what the worksheets are helping the firm develop.

Give Gentle Pokes

As the workshop facilitator it's important to gently question participants on the potential accuracy of the information they are putting on the worksheets. Challenge their assumptions and beliefs. Identify what is based on real data and analysis and what isn't. It's okay to go with gut answers and feelings if the attendees agree. It's all about making conscious decisions.

Here are some questions I find useful when probing ideas and thoughts during the workshop:

> How do you know that's really true?
>
> What would it mean if the opposite was true?
>
> How would a competitor respond to that?
>
> How do you know it exists?
>
> Is there something not being stated?
>
> What is the reason and/or feeling underneath the statement you just made?

Of course, it's the nature of business to operate with an incomplete or less than a perfect set of data; although I encourage good solid research and analysis each company decides for itself how much it needs. Some will operate on gut feel and others will want to get blood tests and finger prints from everyone. Try to find a compromise between the wild pioneer and the one potentially moving towards paralysis by analysis.

As I have mentioned before, it's not unusual to uncover significant business, interdepartmental, or personal issues during a workshop. Some groups may be in full denial of any business problems or blind and deaf to things that challenge their reality. Others may be suffering from an inferiority complex or functioning out of fear. Gentle guiding questions and hypothetical situations are often the best way to expand their view. Sometimes direct assertive statements may be required to bring awareness to an issue. When being direct remember people occasionally follow Newton's third law, "For every reaction there is an equal and opposite reaction."

Worksheet 1 – Business Environment

Business Environment

An Environmental Analysis is a 360° view of the world the firm exists within. It touches on such items as: regulatory bodies and regulations, direct and indirect competitors, economic factors, trends, customer and market perceptions and beliefs, underserved segments, market gaps, distribution, and suppliers. But is it applicable to all firms? What if the firm only makes candy bars, should it still be done? Yes, consider the factors that influence candy sales like the cost of fuel, the price of sugar, disposable income levels, trends towards living a healthier lifestyle, and interest in handcrafted local foods. At the least it causes management to stop, step away from the day-to-day and look at the bigger picture. However, as stated earlier it's beyond the scope of this guide to explain how to do an Environmental Analysis.

The Environmental Analysis serves as input to the SWOT Analysis. The SWOT analysis ends with the selection of an opportunity (brand and/or offering) to pursue in the market. A business should do these at least every two-years. If the firm has already selected an opportunity to pursue, review the information with the group and avoid the temptation to reopen it for discussion. Starting to question the earlier decision can be disruptive to the workshop. However, this can happen regardless of your effort to do otherwise.

If a situation arises where the attendees determine after doing the Environmental and SWOT analysis, the firm needs to pivot from its current path, you will need to determine if going forward will be worthwhile or whether you can proceed in a modified fashion. Even if decision makers are participating in the workshop and agree to pivot, I suggest they only agree provisionally and revisit the item in a week or so. This is the equivalent to sleeping on it.

Side Trip Back to Houses and Brands

What if the firm operates in many different industries or in several areas within an industry, how does this relate to selecting one opportunity on which to base the brand? This goes back to the earlier question regarding where the company falls on the continuum of "house of brands" to "branded house." In the "house of brands" case, and especially if there is a lot of diversity, each product or service stands alone and can be treated like an individual company with respect to this workshop. In other words, each major offering goes through its own workshop. Good news for consultants.

A firm that leans heavily towards a "branded house," focuses more on setting its positioning based on the core competencies its products and services share. However, the more diverse the offerings are the more generalized the firm's overall brand may become. If the firm's offerings are linked by similar technologies, styling, or attributes - related diversity, then the brand expression tends to be less generalized. Where on the continuum should a firm be? That's a strategic decision for the company.

Some car manufactures not known for luxury cars have moved, or are moving, into the luxury car market. Toyota decided they had a low probability of extending their affordable every person's brand of car into the luxury market, so they created Lexus – house of brands. KIA is taking a different approach. At the time of this writing, they are trying to expand into the luxury car market under their current name and brand – branded house. It remains to be seen if the upscale consumer market will support Kia's choice.

After assessing the business environment stop and have a discussion on what this information means with respect to brand definition and development? What is just over the horizon that will influence the strength of the brand or inform how the firm and brand needs to evolve?

Worksheet 1 - Business Environment

1. Core Competencies

What is/are the firm's core competency or competencies? Are any of these unique to the market? Which ones are the most relevant today and to what group? Which ones, if any, could another firm duplicate? Can they be made obsolete?

2. Under Served Segment

Is there a customer segment that has unmet unarticulated or articulated needs? Is a major competitor not responding to customer complaints or desires? Is a part of the market expressing frustration with the status quo? How big is the under-served market? Are there any firms attempting to address this market?

3. Market Gap

Is there a gap in the technology, process, or practice of the market that could provide a viable opportunity? What would the firm or offering need to do to fill this gap? Would this gap be easy for others to fill too? Is there something from another industry that could fill this gap?

4. Relevant Economic Conditions

What are the regional, national, or international conditions that either contribute or inhibit the growth of the market? How will the firm take advantage or mitigate these conditions? Over the next five-years is there a possible economic or trade condition that could help or threaten the firm? What would the early indicators of these be and how could the firm respond?

5. Emerging Trends, Regulations, Issues, or Threats to Market or Industry

Over the next five-years are there any emerging trends, regulations, opportunities, issues, or threats to the market and/or customer base? For example, a government regulation to install a new technology, new emissions restrictions, a disruptive technology, or a new radical business model. Are any of these time bound?

27

Worksheet 1 - Business Environment

1. Core Competencies	2. Under Served Segment

3. Market Gap	4. Relevant Economic Conditions

5. Emerging Trends, Regulations, Issues, or Threats to Market or Industry

Worksheet 2 – SWOT Analysis

It's a Four-Dimensional Assessment

The SWOT Analysis is the business school go to when working on business strategy; however, it's beyond this guide to instruct you on how to do one. There are a lot of references available via the Internet.

The sheet has two major parts. Part one is an assessment on the four SWOT dimensions – two externally and two internally focused. The second is analysis, which ends in selecting an opportunity to pursue to increase the long-term health and viability of the business. This selection should help validate or inform the brand strategy. This sheet is primarily about sharing, it assumes the analysis was done prior to the workshop. However, completing the SWOT during the workshop does occur from time-to-time. If they have completed the traditional SWOT, I then focus entirely on doing a brand SWOT.

Recently, I altered the SWOT structure for workshops at large companies by adding a few extra bits. Under Strength, Weakness and Threats, I have the group look both internally and externally. This can help reveal some additional information. For example, sometimes departments within the firm may be as threatening (uncooperative) as outside forces or resistant to change.

The greatest amount of analysis activity centers on evaluating the list of opportunities to determine the one to pursue. After selecting the opportunity, the firm needs to re-examine the other dimensions to ascertain what may need to be strengthened, eliminated, improved, or added to best support the chosen opportunity. As stated before, I am assuming the firm has already done a SWOT analysis and the opportunity has been selected. In my experience firms generally don't go back to the SWOT after opportunity selection to re-evaluate. I highly suggest going back. Also, once the opportunity is known, then you can do a brand SWOT analysis.

General questions:

- What behaviors will support the selected opportunity?
- What will make the chosen opportunity highly relevant and meaningful to customers?
- Does the selected opportunity enable the firm to establish a mid- to long-term competitive barrier?

Brand SWOT questions:

- What are the brand's strengths? What market, or markets, does the brand appeal to? What factors make this a strong brand? How do you know?
- How does the firm behave its current brand? What factors, experiences, or expectations does the current brand evoke? What customer segment does this brand appeal to?

- Is the brand considered weak? What are the factors that cause the brand to be perceived as weak? What is the firm doing to weaken its brand?

- What changes in the market threaten or will threaten the brand's position? How are competitors threatening the brand? What internal actions are threatening the brand?

- Given the answer to the questions, should the brand be altered, if yes, in what way?

Business Objectives and Strategies

Although these worksheets center on brand they can also help build the firm's operational business objectives. Objectives are outcomes based on time bound measurable goals (search the Internet for information on SMART Goals). For example, "The business will increase earnings by 10% by the end of 2022." An objective does not state how it's achieved. If you find an objective contains words like and, by or through it indicates a strategy is included in the objective. It's best to separate these.

A strategy is a broad statement indicating how a firm will achieve its goal. It isn't specific enough to act on. What makes them actionable are the one to five major tactics associated with them. Typically, each department will have objectives and strategies that support the overall business objectives. Brand and positioning are business strategies.

In vertically integrated firms, one group's business strategy may be rephrased into a lower group's objectives. The group's objective then drives the creation of their strategies and tactics. This cascading process is what guides vertical integration. During the planning workshop this cascade is built up in a stepwise fashion to become a work breakdown structure. I suggest as you create materials in the workshop you build a coding structure like the one listed below to help later planning.

Objective 1
    Strategy A
        Tactic 1
        Tactic 2
    Strategy B
        Tactic 1
        Tactic 2

Objective 2
    Strategy A
        Tactic 1
        Tactic 2
    Strategy B
        Tactic 1
        Tactic 2

Objective 2
    Strategy A
        Tactic 1
        Tactic 2
    Strategy B
        Tactic 1
        Tactic 2

Objective 3
    Strategy A
        Tactic 1
        Tactic 2
    Strategy B
        Tactic 1
        Tactic 2

Worksheet 2 - SWOT Analysis

1. Strenghts	2. Weaknesses
What are the internal and external strengths the firm has and consistently delivers on? How does the firm know this is true?	What are the internal and external weaknesses the firm has and consistently stumbles over or causes it issues in the market? How does the firm know this is true?

3. Opportunities	4. Threats
What opportunities existing in the market that the firm would be able to fill and gain advantage from? Brainstorm a list starting with the existing market segment and then branch out to associated and new industry sectors.	What are the internal and external threats facing the firm? For example, perhaps the pool of talented workers not keeping pace with demand. Are there regulatory or supply threats?

5. Opportunity Selected	What opportunity was selected and why.
6. Strengths Evaluation	Given the opportunity, what items should be left at their current level of strength and which ones should be made even stronger?
7. Weaknesses Evaluation	With respect to the opportunity selecte, what items should be eliminated and which ones should be fixed or strengthened?
8. Threats Evaluation	Given the selected opportunity, are the threats the same? Which threats should be addressed first?

Worksheet 2 - SWOT Analysis

1. Strenghts	2. Weaknesses

3. Opportunities	4. Threats

5. Opportunity Selected	
6. Strengths Evaluation	
7. Weaknesses Evaluation	
8. Threats Evaluation	

Worksheet 3 – Target Customer Segment

"All you need is love…"

What would it be like if the business-customer relationship was built on a healthy loving foundation? No co-dependency, exploitation, or abuse; only a true heart-to-heart connection. The exchange of goods for money (exchange of rings) being a symbol of mutual commitment. How would it feel to experience business in this way? What would a firm built on this basis be like?

It sounds weird, but does it feel true on some level? What would the customer retention rates be if the customer and the firm were in this type of relationship? What would it be like to work for a firm with this attitude? It may appear on the surface the customer only wants the physical thing – candy and flowers, or the company only the money, but isn't there something else, something deeper? Below the obvious is a desire by both for connection and mutual support. When you consider the target customer segment keep this idea in mind. Remember, commerce is people and don't we all want love, respect, belonging, and support?

If your client is open to the idea of becoming a "loving brand" remember, brands are behaved. This means the firm can't be afraid to show love within its walls too. Specifically, unconditional love. Don't confuse unconditional love with the absence of healthy boundaries. A firm does not have to give away the store just because it loves its customers and employees.

What if we replace the "business is war" concept; where we fight over the customer as territory against a competitor, with one that is about helping a customer fulfill their dreams while meeting ours? If we focused on that, would there be a need for war? If our orientation centered on each other's dreams coming true would the customers want to date someone else? Would there be a need to fight over a customer? I believe, a firm constantly focused on staying in sync with the customers' evolving needs and aspirations while maintaining their (the firm's) identity, will experience a long-term stable relationship – little effect from competitors.

Firms and customers, just like everyone else, are looking for that right someone; that good match. This and the next section are about finding the characteristics of the good match as well as forming the basis for a segmentation analysis. The worksheets help define what the firm wants in a perspective customer and what a potential customer wants from the firm. This forms the basis of the business love bond. All this information leads eventually to the design of the brand architecture. The metaphor for this and the next section is a dating service I call dreamprospects.com.

Questions to consider:

- What elements should the brand have that would bring the firm and customer closer together?
- What items or things would irritate or drive a wedge between the firm and the customer?
- What effect should, or shouldn't, the customer's personality have on the firm's brand?

Prior to the workshop you may need to work with the management team, Marketing, Customer Support, and Sales to gather up information on their customers, ex-customers, and lost sales campaigns. If the materials are inadequate or not there you may need to educate them on the need for some research before doing a brand workshop. If this is a new opportunity to the company, then you will need to convince them to do research on the customer segment they believe will be interested in the opportunity selection. Even with good existing research you still may need to do some spot qualitative interviews with customers or potential customers to ascertain what they look for in a firm.

I am the Same – I am Unique

People like to form community. It's part of our hardwiring. Whether it is sports, scrapbooking, comic books, wearing a reptile on a polo shirt, or being a Linux programmer we all want to affiliate with something, especially a winning team or successful brand.

We love to show our colors – our affiliation, to signal to others like us that we belong to the same group and to show those that aren't like us that they don't belong. Luxury brands are great examples of this. Motorcycle owners too; they wave to each other but not to moped riders. When developing the brand consider how the firm will support the formation of a healthy community. Consider the difference between a healthy and unhealthy community from the view of someone inside and outside the group. This will reveal some aspects of the target market and/or aid in the segmentation analysis.

Equally as strong as the need for being part of a community or group is the desire to be recognized as unique and special. When a firm creates its brand, it needs to understand how it will support these two drives: individuality verses group identity and customization verses commonality. How will the brand make the customer feel special and recognize them as being part of a select group?

Experience at Achievement

Block 3.4 is often hard for some people to answer. The focus is not on the item but on what the item lets the customer experience and feel. The answers should be focused on the emotions experienced or the state of being achieved. In other words, "I experience being rich," is okay, but expressing what "being rich" feels like or opens up is more insightful. For example, it may be an experience of feeling safe and secure.

Don't push people too hard on this one, they may feel uncomfortable expressing in this way with the group. Even though they are speaking for a customer they are subconsciously speaking about themselves. For that reason, if possible, it is best to interview selected customers about this item too.

Got Linked?

A brand symbolizes what the firm can do to relieve a customer's tension, conflict, barrier, or to help them achieve an aspiration. This section also explores the customers' needs and what triggers them. Knowing the source of the trigger enables the firm to position its brand as the solution or vehicle to relieve tension or to help attain an aspiration.

Successful linkage between brand, problem and solution means when potential customers experience an issue or need the name of the firm pops into their heads instantly. This is one of the roles of advertising. This is called being "top of mind." Generally, there will be one to three firms holding this position. Companies that are not "top of mind," will find it difficult to compete against those on the list. Creating linkage is one of the major functions of a promotional campaign.

An exercise I recommend is to have the group list who the major competitors are in their market niche', what are they each known for, and what need, problem, or aspiration are each of their brands or offerings linked to. Often, they will list the same things for each one, probe assertively, get them to go deeper to reveal the slight differences between firms. How will this inform the brand definition? In preparation for a workshop I will look at the competitors' websites and promotional materials to develop a sense of how they are positioning themselves. When the group does the exercise, I can then see how much they know about their competitors.

Segmentation Analysis

After this worksheet I talk to the group about segmentation or cluster analysis in preparation for them doing an informal, back of the envelop exercise. I explained this exercise in the pre-worksheet materials of this book. I would still suggest the firm do a formal cluster analysis research study to supplement the exercise here.

Worksheet 3 – Target Customer Segment

1. Firm's Dating Preference

What are the characteristics, attributes, and beliefs the firm desires in its ideal mate, customer? Think about the ideal customers' economic position, social interests, psychological make up, values, culture, talents, motivations or other traits. Which of these items is most important to the firm? Which items does the firm have in common?

2. Customer Desires & Worries

What are the characteristics, attributes, and beliefs of the potential customer relative to the opportunity? Think about the average customer's economic position, social interests, hobbies, psychological make up, values, culture, talents, motivations, and other traits. With respect to the opportunity or offering, what do customers' desire? What is driving this desire? What can the firm do with this information?

3. Customers' Dating Preferences

What are the customers' unarticulated needs with respect to the opportunity and the firm? Describe the characteristics the customers want in their dream date (vendor)? What things have previous vendors done to them that would make customers hesitant to try again, or wish to stay? What does the typical customer need or expect from the firm?

4. Experience at Achievement

What will the customer experience (positive or negative) when they interact with the firm and/or its offerings, or enjoying the promised benefits? Describe this in emotional, psychosocial, aspirational, and/or survival terms. Define the meaning of any key terms. What will the customer do with this experience and/or how will they be changed by it?

5. Motivators

With respect to the selected opportunity, what condition, or conditions, exists that motivates a potential customer to want to start a relationship with the firm? What would friends, family, colleagues, or the media need to say in order to influence a customer to purchase from the firm?

6. Barriers

With respect to the selected opportunity, what condition, or conditions, exists that present barriers to someone or a company starting a relationship with the firm? What are the elements of the opportunity that may be perceived as barriers to purchasing from (marrying) the firm? What would friends, family, colleagues, or media need to say in order to influence a person or company not to purchase from the firm?

Worksheet 3 – Target Customer Segment

1. Firm's Dating Preference

2. Customer Desires & Worries

3. Customers' Dating Preferences

4. Experience at Achievement

5. Motivators

6. Barriers

Worksheet 4: Segment Summary

Have the group look back over the material from Worksheet 3 and focus on the attributes of the customers. As you review the answers with them, help them determine if the attributes and other information described one customer type or more. If all the characteristics are found in one type, then there is a good chance there is only one customer segment. However, even in this case explore, with respect to the opportunity and existing brand, whether there are other significant differences in this single group; for example, culture, location, age, sex, habits or interests, or span of operations that would point to sub-groupings or sub-segments.

As noted earlier in this book, I generally do a segmentation exercise in small groups and try to get them to find new and unique ways to segment their potential customers. Obtaining a new segmentation method can help better inform the positioning of the firm.

It may be helpful to use the questions below to stimulate discussion on customer population segments. These questions help to get at the philosophy and interests of the potential customers. Examine both the positive and negative aspects of these questions. For example, what are the positive attributes and negative attributes of the celebrity choice? How would this play out in a sales campaign? Also, consider the age, economic level, education, and other psychosocial attributes. Do not feel restricted to what is listed below. For B2B think of the companies as individuals.

What celebrity would the customer be?	What foods would he/she like to eat?
What sports would he/she watch?	What type of movie would it enjoy?
What car would it drive?	What do they like to do in their spare time?
What animal would it be?	What do they aspire to?
Where do they operate (local, international)?	What is important to them?
Budget or feature driven?	Traditional or modern (early adopter)?
What is their reputation or brand?	What groups do they belong to?

When you have explored the segment question to your satisfaction complete Worksheet 4

Worksheet 4 – Customer Segment Summary

Item	Primary Segment	Secondary Segment	Tertiary Segment
Segment Name			
Common Behavioral Attributes			
Common Objectives or Goals			
Common Values and Beliefs			
Common Needs			
Motivators			
Barriers			
Other characteristics or attributes in common			

Worksheet 5 – Firm's Personality Defined

Overview

"I can't recognize you, if I can't recognize myself. I can't know you unless I know myself first. I can't love you until I first love myself." - Yitzhak ben Yoel.

The firm needs to know itself, or create itself, before it can truly know what it wants in a customer. These next sheets will begin exploring this idea. At the end of the process the firm will go through an exercise to define its brand personality.

"Do not determine their virtue from their manifesto; the truth is in their actions."
- Yitzhak ben Yoel.

Virtue is the set of behaviors demonstrating one is living to a high standard of moral, ethical, and social conduct. It's generally something we respect in others and aspire to maintain in ourselves. We trust people who act with integrity and virtue and we like doing business with them too. Great brands strive to act with integrity and virtue throughout their organization. Strive, because no one or business is perfect. The management team, like parents with children, have an obligation to model, teach, and coach their organization on virtue and integrity.

It takes years to build trust and integrity in the market and only a moment to tear it down. Market value and brand strength rests on virtue, integrity, relevance, fairness, and consistency; also known as character. There is an old saying, "How a firm behaves when events or things sour speaks volumes about its character." Consider how BP (British Petroleum) first handled the oil spill in the Gulf of Mexico in April 2010. It's a classic case on how *not* to manage a situation and the brand. Of course, there was no way that situation was going to be anything but a wound to the brand, but how big and deep that wound was could have been lessened, if it was managed with more integrity and virtue.

Strong brands, good brands, and great brands consistently exhibit integrity and virtue. These companies go beyond writing corporate manifestos about honesty, integrity, quality, ethics, people first, customer-driven, etc. to teach and live these attributes every day and in every action. These companies believe that acting in conflict to their manifesto increases the likelihood they will fall short of reaching their maximum potential. Do customers prefer a low price from a company that lies and cheats them or would they pay a higher price to work with people they trust? Answer, it depends. Would you like to work for a company that lies and cheats?

The worksheet helps assess the firm's personality, what it believes and values, and whether it holds true to these in day-to-day operations. This is not about looking to blame or judge, rather it's to bring awareness of any disconnects between what is desired and what is practiced. Correcting disconnects strengthens the brand.

It's also about finding out how the firm consciously or unconsciously prioritizes their values. For example, does it appear to the workforce that shipping on time is more important than quality? That can't be true, is states in our corporate handbook that quality is number one. This isn't about what is written, it's about what is really happening on the floor. I have worked with firms that state to the world that quality is their mission, but their internal behaviors revealed they often ship on time at the expense of quality. Firms wanting to create a strong brand ensure their internal operations match their public statements.

Work with these sheets in two steps. First, assess where the firm is today. Second, re-do the sheet from the point of view of what the firm should be like in the future. This second state is the one to build the brand architecture and the firm around.

Values, Disconnects, and Compromises

In the section on values, the focus is on determining the firm's principles or standards of behavior about what is important in life within and surrounding the company as well as what they are doing, rather than saying. If there are disconnects between what is stated and action, it can become a festering wound within a corporate culture and brand.

Disconnects occur when the firm repeatedly violates its beliefs or values and/or causes employees to be in conflict with their personal integrity. People will generally try to relieve this conflict, or stress by quitting, causing disruption, reducing productivity, wrecking the customer experience, disassociating from themselves at work, or potentially doing physical damage to the company. Disconnects create ripples of instability in the firm and a loss of respect in management. If these go on long enough they may become embedded in the firm's processes and culture either formally or informally.

Look for these in you pre-work and during the workshop. Bring them to the surface in a compassionate way. It's their choice to change or not.

In the compromise block we begin exploring the operational and behavioral limits of the firm with respect to its day-to-day activities. How do the answers in this block impact the selected opportunity and the target customer segment? Compromise in this context is about settling for something less than desired or planned (not a win/win). A similar exercise is run for items that are sacred to the firm.

What we hold sacred is truly one of the defining items of the brand. If the firm holds concepts like contemporary design, environmental responsibility, or affordable living as sacred this will become the touchstone that guides the viewpoint and choices of the company. Sacred items are part of the brand architecture and generally show up as one or more pillars.

Why all this stuff on values, compromising, etc.? Simply it's a way to shine a mirror on the firm and give it a chance to become more aware of itself and see where it can improve to become a better match for the customers. Marketing meets the human potential movement.

Heroes and Allies

We use the heroes block to begin assessing the character traits of the firm, and later with other inputs, to help inform the choice of sensory elements for expressing the brand. How do these traits align with the target customer segment?

Allies are those non-customers that believe in the firm; provide aid, and who the firm has a relationship with and obligation to support. They can also help multiple the effects of the firm's promotional efforts by echoing the company's messages. Oh, and they are not afraid to whack the firm upside the head when they don't see reality.

Raison d'Être – Reason for Being

This is very important to this process. What is the firm's reason for being? Why is it in business? Take the following off the table before asking for answers: making money, keeping the customer happy, beating the competition, and shareholder value. Ask them to go deep. How does the firm want to change the world, support people, achieve its own motivation, etc.? This is an integral part of the brand.

Worksheet 5 – Firm's Personality

1. Values

What are the firm's values – principles or standards of behavior? What are the firm's fundamental beliefs? How does the firm act on these beliefs? What value or values would the firm choose to go out of business over rather than to violate?

2. Compromises

Has the firm ever violated one more of its values? If yes, which one, or ones, and why? Are there any policies or practices within the firm that managers and the workforce regularly ignore? When would lying to a customer or the workforce be okay?

3. Sacred

What does the firm hold as sacred? Consider this from many different angles, for example, design, politics, spirituality, human resources, sourcing, utility, sourcing, deployment, or quality.

4. Heroes

What real, fictional, or mythical heroes best represents the firm? What are the positive and negative traits they share with the firm? Is this the right hero or heroes to stand for the brand? If not, what hero should it be and which of the hero's characteristics should the firm emulate?

5. Allies

Who or what are the firm's allies? How do you know they are allies? What do the allies provide the firm? What character traits and beliefs does the firm and the allies have in common? How does this alliance influence the brand?

6. Raison d'Être

Why is the firm in business? What is its reason for being? How is it going to change the world, an industry, or the human condition? How does it bring light into the world? How does the firm know when it has achieved it raison d'être? What then?

Worksheet 5 – Firm's Personality

1. Values	2. Compromises
3. Sacred	4. Heroes
5. Allies	6. Raison d'Être

Worksheet 6: DreamProspects.com

The exercise on this worksheet is to begin setting up for the transition from gathering information to making the final push to defining the brand. The concept focuses on an online dating site metaphor, DreamProspects.com

Sales are a lot like dating, isn't it? Picture the firm as a person. Who would it be? What would it be like? When the firm walks into a party what are people thinking when they see him/her? It may seem like the previous sheets have covered this, and it's true to some extent; however, this helps add more dimension. Be creative relative to the information already gathered.

Refer to the previous worksheets to complete 6.1 through 6.3. Complete blocks 6.4 by listing as many one or two-word descriptive phrases as possible about the firm. Focus on using active, dynamic, and emotional words and avoid corporate-speak. These will be used in block 6.5.

Have them work individually first then they can return to small groups to create one compelling profile. They can start with as long and rich a profile as they wish and then it needs to be edited down to seventy-five words or less. Help them avoid getting caught in an endless refinement loop – good enough is fine. Coach them on avoiding diluting the message down to make everyone happy. Try to ensure those with weak voices get heard in this process.

Worksheet 6 – Firm's Dating Profile

1. Core beliefs and values	2. Most Attractive Features

3. Must haves in a mate?	4. Active, dynamic, and emotional phrases that describe the firm

5. Using previous blocks and sheets, write a dating profile for the firm to attract the primary customer segment (75 words or less).

Worksheet 7 – Courtship

A Little More Love…

"Win customers for life. Delight the customer. The customer is first. Make the customer feel special. It starts with the customer and ends with the customer. We pride ourselves on having great customer relationships." - Typical business clichés

These taglines are common in B2B and B2C enterprises, yet they don't truly touch on the essence of what is underneath. Perhaps as business people we are afraid to use the right term – it can be scary to use the L-word; love.

Some firms say, "We love our customers," but for a few companies this sentence is missing an unspoken insidious addition; "*…as long as they are purchasing from us*." This is conditional love. If they stop buying, we don't love them anymore. The firm may even feel angry, rejected, abandoned, inadequate, and/or fearful. The phrase "it's not personal; it's business," is a fallacy, everything is personal; companies are made of people. Ever want to get back at an ex-customer? It's all personal, isn't it. Of course, it doesn't have to be.

What would it be like if the sentence, "We love our customers," is changed to, "We are in love with our customers?" This turn of phrase is to denote an unconditional love that seeks connection whether a transaction occurs or not. It's also an understanding that by expressing love in all dealings, even when a purchase doesn't occur, the goodwill and positive energy projected by the "love-firm," may set up a better future state with the individual and/or those they influence. Some say, "What goes around comes around," and whether it's true or not, acting as if it's true helps make the world a happier place. Again, let's dropped the whole business is war thing.

Unconditional love does not mean subsuming the needs and feelings of the firm to the customer or vice versa. It requires loving the person as they are; their essence, as an equal. It includes supporting each other in growing and prospering in healthy ways. Sometimes it's loving their essence even when their ways and yours don't align enough to have any type of relationship.

Like all relationships a business can't truly practice unconditional love unless it first has unconditional love for itself. Can a firm express love for its customers if it doesn't express love within its four walls? My advice is to model inside the company the behaviors customers should experience at the front of the store. This is one of the contexts to keep in mind as the brand is designed, that is, inside behaviors drive the outside expression of the brand. This helps create a business that people want to connect with and help build.

As the facilitator, you can help them understand and apply this love concept into their brand and their firm's behaviors. It may be a real shock to some companies that have always thought of their actions in terms of power, exploitation, and privilege.

Some items to consider when later formulating the firm's brand behaviors, or culture:

- Engage fully with each other - be 100% focus in that moment
- Practice open and honest communication from a place of love and empathy
- Speak one's truth from a place of personal responsibility and integrity
- Listen to understand, in contrast to listening to formulate a reply
- Realize that everyone is doing the best they can at every given moment, and when they know more and/or are more aware they will do better.
- Hold each other and the customers 100% responsible for their own actions, feelings, and reactions.
- Express one's concerns, hurts, and boundaries in a healthy way and support others doing the same
- Embrace differences; it opens the mind and is good for business
- Foster trust – forgive freely
- Never compromise the individual's or the firm's integrity
- Contribute to building mutually supporting relationships
- Break off relationships that aren't healthy
- Be free to be who you are
- Cultivate patience, understanding, and flexibility in dealings.
- Build community
- Don't cultivate or support a victim mindset
- Love for the joy of loving – no strings, no expectations, no guilt or shame, and no conditions

Intersection and Commonality

This section is a further exploration of what was started on earlier sheets. We tend to form relationship easier with those whose beliefs, personality, values, desires, etc. intersect with our own. We may also bond over a common experience or interest; however, some bonds carry a potential negative shadow. For example, a bond formed over a trauma or dependency. Avoid creating dependent customers; they eventually revolt. This also refers to items the firm and customer intersect on and do act on as well as not acting on in a common way. It is important to probe this area.

Just for Them – A Special Gift

When the firm intersects and understands its target customers then it can deliver them a gift that is deeply meaningful and memorable. The gifts are the firm's offerings. Great brands design offerings that meet the customers' articulated and some of their key unarticulated (latent) needs. Delivering on unarticulated needs can generate fantastic customer loyalty and differentiation.

Suitors

This section begins the discussion that will lead to identifying the sustainable competitive differentiator. It may be worthwhile to consider Porter's Forces here as well. The objective is to think about the elements of the brand that could render the competitor invisible to a loyal customer. I often offer a follow-up workshop six-months after this one called "Customer Loyalty by Design." It's built on the premise that knowing my brand and my target customers I can design my offerings and process to create loyalty on first use of the product. This idea results in a higher resistance to suitors by the customer base.

Worksheet 7 – Courtship

1. Intersection & Commonality

List the major items, issues, or beliefs the firm needs to, or has, intersection on, or commonality with, the target customer segment? 7.1B. Are there any items the firm doesn't align with that will impact the success or the brand of the firm? If yes, how will his be addressed?

2. Just for Them

Answer these questions for each column below.

What would make the firm's brand (offering) a meaningful or magical gift to the target customer base with respect to the selected opportunity? List the key elements of this experience? What makes this experience unique from the competition?

Offering Impact	Brand Impact

3. Suitors

What makes the competitors a threat to your current or potential relationship with the customers? How do you know it is a threat? What will the firm do to minimize these threats from competitors?

4. Show the Love

What attributes, elements, concepts, or feelings does the brand need to express to demonstrate its unconditional love for the market? How does the customer know that the firm has unconditional love for them? How will "show the love," impact the firm's processes, offerings, and hiring of talent?

Copyright 2027 David Okent. All rights reserved worldwide. www.okentconsultingservices.com

Worksheet 7 – Courtship

2. Just for Them

Offering Impact	Brand Impact

1. Intersection & Commonality

3. Suitors

4. Show the Love

Worksheet 8 – Differentiation

Darwin brought back many specimens from his trips and the most famous ones were from the Galapagos. Years after the trip experts re-examined many of his Galapagos bird specimens and determined a number identified as different, unique were in fact all finches. Over eons, groups of these finches physically adapted to different food sources. Same basic bird, but having different beaks and other physical attributes specialized to their specific food choice.

Nature, the great free market, used natural selection to shape each group of finches to best fit their food source or niche. This shaping or differentiation enabled the finches to minimize potential conflict between groups and others. Businesses are the same; they attempt to minimize competition for customers by differentiating to serve different customer segments (food sources). In addition, differentiation is not static, it needs to evolve in response to changes in the customer segment as well as to adapt to pressure from competitors (predators).

Unlike finches, businesses can decide to strike a balance between specialization by form, fit, and function and being flexible and adaptable. This balance helps prevent waking up to find the customer base gone. Ideally, it's best to be in sync with the food source or to be ready to switch to another type of food if the current source is dwindling. This is not in conflict with loving a customer; it ensures there will always be a customer to love. We can still love our ex-customers as we begin to develop relationships with a new segment. We have an unlimited capacity to love. Yes, I'm bouncing between metaphors here.

Differentiation Effects Margin

Differentiation can come in several forms; for example, price, features or functions, outcome, or values and beliefs. Competing on price generally means the firm's and its competitor's offerings are viewed by the market as essentially the same. When this occurs one firm will decide to differentiate by being the lowest priced. Generally, lower margins. Lowest price differentiation demands aggressive supplier management and continuous attention to cutting or stabilizing production and overhead costs.

Differentiating with additional features, functions, or lower risk (a type of feature) in contrast to the competitor's offering supports a higher price relative to price positioning. This is assuming the added features generate benefits that are relevant to the customer. As a general category, toothpaste is a good example of differentiation by feature. Toothpastes all have the same basic function and the only thing that competitors can differ on are things like taste, texture, whitening, tarter control, abrasiveness, color, and packaging. Of course, some brands of toothpaste compete on lowest price, others by appealing to certain ages, a number on health features, and still more on social attributes.

The next up on the value verses differentiation ladder is aspirational outcome. For example, a luxury brand is built and positioned to support a market segment that wants to indicate to themselves and others that they have reached a level of success or exclusivity that few can match. The more a product supports this idea over its competition the higher the price and margin it can command. This assumes the product has some attribute, or attributes, that enable it to claim the luxury space with respect to the perspective of its customers.

The highest value generated by differentiation is by attaching to something of deep meaning (based in values and beliefs) to the customer segment. Owning the product becomes a symbol of what they hold dear or believe. For example, an environmentalist who buys an electric car or someone committed to only buying from stores that support fair trade and organic foods. This level of differentiation commands the highest level of loyalty with the customer and the best margins relative to a competitor not positioning in this way.

Between two firm's competing for the same segment using the deep meaning strategy, the one that attaches more strongly to the customers' belief or adds an additional significant differentiator through outcome or feature will generally obtain the higher market share. This goes for those competing on outcome, they can add feature or price differentiation too.

The best differentiators are those that create a significant barrier to entry, that is, some element that is difficult to duplicate by competitors and other potential predators. The brand identity helps potential customers recall the firm's sustainable competitive difference and how it relates to the customer's need or desire (remember linkage).

A firm's differentiation strategy can be found in such places as their press releases, advertising, packaging, executive statements or interviews, R&D spending allocations, merger activity, annual reports, and new product announcements. It also helps to talk to customers and find out what products they buy and why. This is one area that can't be kept secret for long.

First-Mover Differentiation

There are special times in the history of commerce when a company can create a completely new category, for example: in-line skates, a method for exchanging and viewing multi-media via a computer network – a Browser, or a smart phone. This creates a paradigm shift in the market and for a significant period can allow the firm to graze peacefully alone in a wide-open pasture. This is the first-mover advantage or differentiation by disruption or innovation.

The upside is the firm is alone and free to create the market. The downside is they must invest a significant amount of money to create the market for the product. Roller Blades invested in creating the in-line skate market. The second company into their space harvested Roller Blades' investment in market creation. They didn't have to educate the market or invent a sport, it was already there. Roller Blades didn't have a barrier to entry, only a first-mover advantage.

How does a first-mover not go by the way of Roller Blades or Netscape? Unless they have a solid barrier to entry they should assume they will not be alone for long and begin innovating at a rate ahead of potential newcomers. The incumbent can potentially keep upping the bar to force the newcomers to play catch up. Alternatively, a newcomer can try to reinvent the category by making another disruptive leap or switch to a low-cost strategy. The circle of life.

The Firm's Differentiation Strategy

There isn't much more to say about differentiation that hasn't already been said in this guide; however, three items need to be emphasized, repeated. First, don't accept the team's first couple of answers on differentiation. Acknowledge them and their work, discuss the items briefly, and then have the teams try again; perhaps two or three times. Help them determine if their market uniqueness is truly worthwhile to their target market. It might be great to have a significant sustainable competitive differentiation from your patented production process, but if it isn't recognized as important to the potential customer, then find something else to lead with in the market. Second, once the strategy is determined, test it by reading it with the name of each major competitor. If it sounds true then start again, unless the team wants to compete on the same item. Lastly, check if it's a sustainable competitive advantage. Is it easily copied or difficult to overcome or out flank? If the advantage doesn't create a barrier to entry for competition, this is okay if the firm is aware of it and plans to keep innovating before the competition catches up.

Future History

Future histories are fun, time consuming, and insightful. The future history is a device for establishing a description of the firm's future successful state. We typically select a date twenty-years in the future and tell attendees that all obstacles were overcome. It seems two decades is enough for most people to accept the premise.

Generally, this activity is done as a separate worksheet, but for this guide we combined it with the differentiation strategy materials. It can also be moved to after the Purpose worksheet. However, I like it here because it can reveal the purpose, mission, and vision as a natural by-product.

I tell attendees to write Future Histories of about three to six paragraphs and then to share them with their team. Next, the team writes a "best of" they will later share with the room. Before the team sharing, I may hand out a tip sheet to help them create their history. The tip sheet will ask them to touch on the customers' view, competitors' impact, suppliers, etc., to help round out the picture. Some people may be uncomfortable with writing, that's okay, let them draw a picture. The creation of the "to-be" condition is one of the first steps in doing road mapping, or long-term planning.

Have the small teams develop a list of the ten or twelve most emotive, descriptive, illustrative, and powerful words they can farm from their individual histories. Bring the teams back to together to share, combine, and consolidate their words into fifteen or twenty words or phrases. This is the list call the "words to use." This is the beginning of the new brand language.

Worksheet 8 – Differentiation

1. Competitors' Differentiation

Competitor 1	Competitor 1	Competitor 1
What customer segment are they trying to attract? What issue or aspiration have they linked their brand to? Why do customers purchase from them?		

2. Firm's Differentiation

What items, behaviors, and/or position will the firm use to differentiate itself from others? How will the competitors respond to this differentiation? What makes it import to customers?

3. Future History

Assume it is twenty years in the future and everything that the firm wanted to accomplish relative to the opportunity and its brand has been achieved. From the perspective of a person outside the firm write a brief entry in the "Encyclopedia (Wiki) of Business" about the firm from this future vantage point. How did the firm change the world, an industry, or individuals? What would customers, competitors, business leaders, and others say about the firm? What was/is the firm's brand and value proposition?

Worksheet 8 – Differentiation

1. Competitors' Differentiation

	Competitor 1	Competitor 1	Competitor 1
What customer segment are they trying to attract? What issue or aspiration have they linked their brand to? Why do customers purchase from them?			

2. Firm's Differentiation

3. Future History

Worksheet 9 – Purpose

Overview

Often companies start by formulating their purpose, vision, and mission statements before they do any other planning work. Of course, this isn't the process used here. I prefer to start by understanding the business environment, the competitive strategy, then selecting an opportunity, identifying the target customers, and so on before working on the purpose, vision, mission, and brand. However, it's fine to start with the purpose etc. first and use these to guide the rest of the work. I do it differently because I prefer to be open to possibilities and pivots in the early stages of the process.

Established firms may state they already know their purpose, vision, and mission; therefore, they tend to skip ahead and forgo this work. That's their choice; however, it may be very illuminating to do these pages anyway. If they complete the worksheet they will either validate what they know or find out they need to adjust.

If the company is large and made up of several separate business units the parent company's purpose, vision, and mission statements may be very high level or abstract. This occurs, because the firm is trying to make one statement cover all their operations. The higher the firm's level of diversification the vaguer and more abstract these statements become. This can often make converting the brand statement into behaviors difficult. One solution is to define the high-level cross-enterprise values, culture, etc. the workforce will follow, and then to create a specific set of brand behaviors to address a given offering and/or industry segment.

Why, How, and What

Behind this section and parts of others is an old strategy used to help develop the brand that Simon Sinek made popular in his book and talks called "Start with Why." Until he named it we didn't know it had a name. Congratulations, Simon! Okay, I admit I am a little envious of your success; alright jealous, but I am working on letting these feelings go.

What is the highest level of differentiation that generally supports the best margins? It's meaning. People like to join with those that have similar beliefs, goals, and needs; therefore, don't lead by selling the trinket, start by talking about what the firm believes and why it's in business. Connection through mutual beliefs helps create a spirit-to-spirit bond; in contrast to a trinket-to-wallet relationship.

- Why is the firm in business (answered earlier)?
- How does the firm achieve its purpose?
- What does the firm offer that expresses this uniqueness (differentiation)?

Purpose, Vision, and Mission

My process has specific meanings for purpose, vision, and mission that may not align with some organizations. I won't be so judgmental as to say I am right, but I highly suggest for these worksheets my definitions are followed. Okay, I am judgmental; I am a right.

Purpose is a simple direct statement of why the firm exists. Refer to Worksheet 5.6. Remember profit is not an ideal reason, it's only a metric or a measure. Perhaps the firm exists so a group of creative people can do fun stuff together, while making a living doing it. That's fine. Honestly is good. Maybe the firm's purpose is to give the world a healthy delicious alternative to candy, create safer water, or cut silicon wafer production's impact on the environment. Just keep it simple. If it goes into more than two sentences, try again. The longer it is the less one has a clear idea. My purpose is to help businesses feed more people – to grow and increase their workforce. My mission, how I will accomplish my purpose, is to teach businesses how to do this in healthy, responsible, and sustainable ways.

The vision is a concise statement of what the world is like when the purpose is fulfilled. This is the new bliss created by the firm when it achieves its purpose. Refer to the Future History worksheet. Every employee needs to understand and buy into the purpose and vision to create an optimal system.

Next are the major strategies, the broad statements on how the purpose will be achieved. These broad business strategies will later help generate departmental or functional business objectives that in turn will generate more specific strategies to drive the creation of tactics.

The mission statement is often confused with the purpose statement. The mission is focused on the one pivotal strategy that must be done to attain the purpose. If the firm is a department store that is competing on lowest price then it may have a mission like, "Our mission is to squeeze every penny of cost out of our supply chain." Do you see a relationship between differentiation and mission?

Quality and Great Customer Service

What if the purpose is about having the highest quality, best customer service, or the like? These can be fine, but it's best to check to see if the item is a real purpose by asking, "What end is served by the firm's purpose being [insert item, for example, highest quality], or "Why is [item] important?" The answer to these questions can help determine whether it's a true purpose or a strategy for achieving a purpose. A purpose that reflects the firm's reason for being.

Purpose Statement Examples

These purpose statements below were taken from their websites. Some of these are labeled on their websites as purpose and others as mission statements. The difference between the two with respect to this workshop is mission statements expresses the key strategy. For example, Starbucks shows its strategy after the hyphen, while Burger King shows its starting with "…all freshly." Strategies in purpose or mission statements generally contain a hyphen, semicolon, or connecting words like by, in, and, with, through, and based on. It is best to keep purpose and mission statements separate for clarity.

Starbucks:

To inspire and nurture the human spirit – one person, one cup and one neighborhood at a time.

Burger King:

We proudly serve the best burgers in the business, plus a variety of real, authentic foods…all freshly prepared…just the way you want it.

The Boeing Company Vision:

People working together as a global enterprise for aerospace industry leadership.

Airbus Group:

Airbus Group aims for leadership of the commercial aeronautics and defense and space markets, based on its strong European heritage.

Microsoft:

Our mission is enable people and businesses throughout the world to realize their full potential by creating technology that transforms the way people work, play, and communicate.

Medtronic:

To contribute to human welfare by application of biomedical engineering in the research, design, manufacture, and sale of instruments or appliances that alleviate pain, restore health, and extend life.

Torie & Howard Candies:

We believe that food tastes better when it is made with organic, natural ingredients and responsible principles. We strive to create delicious, tasty treats that are made in a way that is as health-friendly, eco-friendly and socially conscious as possible.

BMW Automobile:

Sheer driving pleasure. Sporting and dynamic performance combined with superb design and exclusive quality.

As I stated before, when companies expand into different industries or contain a number of businesses their purpose, mission, and vision statements tend to become very generalized and similar to their competitors. A good example of this is the Airbus and Boeing statements above. In these cases, expressions of differentiation are often focused on a specific product or service brand.

Worksheet 9 – Vision, Purpose, Mission

1. Purpose Statement

What is the primary purpose of the firm relative to the selected opportunity and the brand? What makes this purpose relevant to the market and/or the target customer segment? Write a concise purpose statement for the workforce.

2. Vision

Write a vision statement that describes the world that results (from the perspective of either the firm, customers, people, industry, country, or the world) from the firm fulfilling its purpose.

3. Objectives

Develop a series of business and/or brand objectives from the vision statement.

4. Strategies (1-2 per Objective)

Define a couple of high-level strategies (broad statements) to achieve the objective relative to the brand

4. Mission Statement

What strategy or strategies, but limit it to two, are pivotal for enabling the firm's purpose and vision. If the item isn't address failure is certain.

Worksheet 9 – Vision, Purpose, Mission

1. Purpose Statement

2. Vision

3. Objectives

4. Strategies (1-2 per Objective)

4. Mission Statement

Worksheet 10 – Brand Architecture

A Promise Supported by Pillars

I already stated the brand is operationalized using a series of behaviors expressed through the firm's people, processes, and offerings. The previous materials hinted that these behaviors spring from the company's purpose, values, competitive position, and differentiation. What organizes these behaviors into a cohesive set is the Brand Architecture.

The Brand Architecture grabs the bits and pieces and glues them together into a coherent whole that eventually guides the development of the firm. The first piece is the brand promise. The promise is the purpose, or the competitive differentiator rewritten as a commitment or outcome to the target customer segment. Walmart's slogan or tagline, "Save money, live better," is an expression of their brand promise.

How does Walmart save people money, so they can live better? That's where the pillars come in. The pillars are the three to five strategies enabling Walmart to make good on their promise. We don't know what they use, but they could have something like highly managed supply chains, shared risk, friendly service, and everything a family needs. Another company may have pillars like bold leadership, relentless relevant innovation, beautiful efficiency, and trusted partner to support a promise like, "Breakthrough products that revolutionize our industry." Notice these strategies are summarized in two- or three-word phrases.

The pillars drive the structure, processes, and behaviors of the firm through the continual refrain of the question, "How can the organization fulfill this pillar? "

Not shown on the worksheet is an exercise I do after the brand pillars are established. We have small teams go off and write one to two paragraphs that explain how each pillar supports the brand promise and the firm's personality. Then each team shares their narrative for the first pillar, which is followed by a group discussion to help come to a common understanding. Then we do the second pillar using the same process and so forth. These short explanations of the pillars will become part of the architecture and more importantly part of the brand education process.

One interesting test is to give someone not involved in this process the brand pillar narratives without an indication of what the actual pillar title is and have him/her summarize the narrative using a phrase of one to three words. It's a great feeling when the reader deduces the pillar title.

Linkage

This is obtained from an earlier worksheet. It is also a time to review and see if it's still valid or needs some refinement. What problem, need, conflict, or desire will the firm's brand be associated to? This helps inform the promotional strategy as well as business development.

Behavioral and Operational Attributes

Just as the pillars are the key to making the promise become true, the behavioral and operational attributes enable fulfilling the pillar. Another way of looking at this is the brand promise is the objective, the pillars are the strategies, and the attributes are the major tactics.

Originally, I didn't draw a distinction between behaviors and operational attributes during workshops. They were just lumped together. Now I try to do these as two separate exercises. But it can still be combined, but the separation occurs after the workshop.

First, assign a pillar to each individual team and ask them to brainstorm the attributes that create it. These are one- or three-word phrases. Have them list as many phrases as they can in five to ten minutes. To help get things started, provide a few examples of attributes that may go under a pillar. Don't forget non-corporate speak attributes like fun, stylish, geeky, hip, tough, soft, compassionate or other dynamic and illustrative terms.

Then have the team select the top ten or twelve phrases that support the pillar, with emphasis of course on the most active, emotive, and dynamic attributes in the list. Next, they return to the larger group to share and discuss their findings. After sharing, the group selects the top five to eight attributes per pillar from all lists. Lastly, we have the group take five minutes to assign as many of the remaining terms to one of the top selected attributes. Some of these left-over items may not fit with any of the chosen or selected attributes just move them to the words-to-use list discussed earlier.

Follow the same process for the operational items, except don't limit the phrases to one- or two-words. Instead prompt for an actual name or very short description of the process or item. These lists are used with later worksheets.

Worksheet 10 – Brand Architecture

1. Brand Promise

Write a short brand promise that will resonate with the target customer segment. Look back and Worksheet 9 and determine if the strategies support this promise. Adjust as needed.

2. Linked Problem

What problem, conflict, tension, aspiration, need, or want will the brand be positioned to resolve, or linked to? How will the firm resolve the issue?

3. Pillars

The brand promise is supported by three to five brand pillars. These are the key strategies and/or differentiators that must be acted on consistently to deliver the promise.

4. Behavioral Attributes

These are the behaviors that define how the firm operates, designs, and works that make the pillars true.

5. Operational Attributes

These are similar to behaviors, but are focused on the processes and functions within the firm that will make the pillars true.

66

Worksheet 10 – Brand Architecture

1. Brand Promise

2. Linked Problem

3. Pillars

4. Behavioral Attributes

5. Operational Attributes

Worksheet 11 - Documenting the Brand Architecture- Part 1

This is a great time to stop and formally document where things now stand. Below is a format I use. The example is for a fictitious B2B company. The operational items have been omitted but they follow the same table layout as the behavioral attributes. Notice the attribute "practical" is part of the Innovation pillar, this is a yin/yang grouping. The behaviors attached to "being practical" help shift the focus from pure to applied research and development, it informs the investment allocation to favor a mix that is more market driven than market driving, and reins in the wild west of "adventurous," with the assistance of disciplined processes.

Brand Pillar #1: Relentless Relevant Innovation

Pillar Narrative (listed earlier as an option): We are adventurous explorers determined to fulfill our need to create, invent, and commercialize revolutionizing technologies, methods, and practices that advance our industry, demonstrates our love and commitment for our customers, and periodically make history.

Attributes

Determined	Targeted	Adventurous	Practical
• Persistent • Goal Oriented • Respectful • Engaged • Navigate • Confident • Negotiate • Assertive	• Industry - Customer Knowledge • Customer driven and customer driving • Accountable • Responsible • Responsive • User-centric	• Fearless • Seeker – Explorer • Experimenter • Imaginative • Finds a Way • Willing to Change • Limitless • Open	• Disciplined Processes • Consistent Rules • Achievable Goals • Synergies • Competitive • Learns • Balanced

The items not selected as one of the major attributes (previous worksheet) are assigned, if possible, to one of the chosen attributes. Not all attributes will find a home under one of the chosen ones, but don't discard items, they are important too.

The Pillar Narrative captures the spirit and intent of the strategy from the workforce's perspective. Writing from the workforce's point of view helps with education and implementation later. Below is another example of a pillar narrative. Imagine how that paragraph might impact the day-to-day operations of the firm. At least one of the pillars should address the key competitive differentiator.

One Community	We are a community of teams and individuals that together support and coach each other in achieving our purpose and our need to learn and grow. Individually and within our teams we help to ensure the group's integrity and ethics. We honor each person simply for who they are, and we understand that everyone is always contributing the best they can to the mission.

Grab some paper and create worksheet 11.

Worksheet 12 - Behavioral and Operational Attribute Narratives

Now as the end of the process approaches everything is starting to fall in place. This next step transforms the brand strategy and architecture into the major tactics and actions that will make the brand real. These narratives will eventually become the seeds for items like the product and service design principles and the organizational, behavioral, and operational tactics that form the firm's culture. The output of this work may be used in another exercise to create a road map to the new brand's end state.

The key to this section is asking, "How does the firm, department or team behave or operationalize the attribute of [fill in the blank]?" Don't expect to get a highly polished finish on this first draft. The polishing process will take some time to complete.

Generally, I have the participants break into their small teams and take about 30 minutes to write a first draft of a narrative for a chosen attribute and its group. Although challenging, an extra credit process is to have all the small teams write a narrative for each grouping (that can take two or three hours, not including breaks). When doing the extra credit process spend time comparing and discussing the differences between the team's write-ups. Alternatively, you can assign one attribute group to each team and then share and discuss the team outputs in the total group.

Here are some questions to help get the small groups thinking:

- How can an organization be [insert attribute]?
- How do employees show they understand what [attribute] means?
- How can the level of [attribute] be measured?
- How does management support [attribute]?
- What is the up side of this [attribute] and how it is expressed?
- What is the downside and how will that be mitigated?
- What part of [attribute] will the customer experience?
- How is the [attribute] embedded in the offerings?

The other helpful tip for writing narratives is to give the small teams a point of view or "who's talking to whom" to help them frame their writing. The other important items are: 1) use as many or all the attributes assigned to the group in the narrative, and 2) if other attributes are needed go ahead and add them. A good narrative illuminates the business structure and the tactics that support it.

Below is an example of a write up for "Adventurous." Each narrative is written as if the brand is fully in place and successful. Each narrative is created without consideration to the other narratives. When all the narratives are completed they are read together against the brand structure and adjusted as needed. This example does not include the operational attributes.

Example - Adventurous

"We are fearless innovators who are ready to try new things, to change and evolve with the times, and are open and encouraging of imagination and new paradigms. Our culture balances the current mission needs with a commitment to give each other time to think, explore, express, create, and invent. We invest in learning and tools to support experimentation and development.

Our environment is open, collaborative, and strives to be limitless. We celebrate pushing the boundaries of "what is" regardless of success or failure. Our motto, "It's better to try and fail than not to have tried at all."' We do strive to be limitless, but recognize resources aren't; therefore, we manage our resources appropriately and ensure our work will benefit the market.

Our organization is aware of the advancements going on outside our company and industry and we find ways to incorporate the best of these into our designs and processes. However, we are explorers, pioneers, and inventors first and farmers second."

Given the narrative above, is it possible to use those three paragraphs to help guide the development of the corporate culture, hiring process, and other business strategies and tactics? How would a manager lead, manage and hire given this attribute? What questions would you ask someone in an interview to see if they would be a good fit for this attribute? If the entire firm was built around this one attribute would it be optimal? If yes, how would this create an optimal environment? If no, what other attribute, or attributes, are needed to achieve an optimal condition? Does the attribute narrative support the brand promise it stems from, that is, "delivering breakthrough products that revolutionize the industry?"

Here are some more helpful questions:

- What aspects of the narrative directly support the brand promise?
- Which items help other items support the promise?
- What items are needed, but don't impact the promise?

A Peak at Implementation

At this point in the process, the pillars and behavioral and operational narratives cover the overall direction of the enterprise. However, the enterprise-level behavioral and operational attributes and narratives may not be focused enough for individual departments to implement. During the implementation process, individual departments and some key teams use the enterprise structure as a starting point to create their group's specific attribute list and narratives to act on.

This can feel a bit overwhelming for medium to large firms, but there are two ways to make this easier. Both methods start with educating management and the workforce on the business objectives, strategies, brand position, and architecture (including the existing narratives), and what their role is in making this structure real.

The first method is to have each department compose their own team specific behavioral and operational attributes and narratives based on the firm's new brand pillars. The advantage of this method is everyone is moving at the same pace together towards attaining a strong vertically integrated organization. The second method focuses on building momentum for change through small victories in contrast to the first that favors having everything fully defined before change can begin. Maybe this is like Waterfall Verses Agile in the software industry.

The second method asks each manager and their team to learn and understand the pillars and the pillar narratives and then to identify one thing they can do within the next three-to-six months to make one of the pillars real or stronger. As the team works on this item, the management team completes the first method (top down). If the management team isn't done when the team's item is completed the team selects a second item to work on. Again, they rely on their own interpretation of the pillar narrative to select an action. Once the team members know the direction they usually will make good project selections. The key is to make sure this one item is in the team's control.

An orientation that can help a team with this concept is for the workgroup to consider themselves a business; where the groups that provide materials or information to them are vendors and those they serve are their customers. They work with their vendors to ensure they get their own needs met, and then work with their customers (the group they hand-off to) to enable them to be successful in their contribution to the brand.

Some departments, like finance, may not need to take the process very deep, but the rule of thumb here is the closer a group is to the customer (for example, sales, product development, or service) the more extensive and detailed are the list of brand tactics.

Gather up all the attributes that were under the attribute categories and begin writing a narrative explanation of what the category means from an operational and/or experiential perspective. Try to incorporate as many of the attributes within a category as possible. After reading this narrative would it be possible for a management team to create an organizational structure, process, or set of principles to make this true? Attribute narratives are a pivotal step to making the brand a reality. Use this sheet as stimulus to write the narratives. Use a format like the one below to record the information.

Example of Worksheet 12:

Pillar Name	
Behavioral and Operational Attribute	Narrative
Behavior Title	
Behavior Title	
Behavior etc.	
Operational Title	
Operational Title	
Operational etc.	

Worksheet 13 - Documenting the Architecture: Part 2

In part 2, the focus is on formally documenting the entire architecture. For simplicity (laziness?), I am not showing it completely filled-out, instead I have put in placeholders to help show the format. This format is followed for each pillar and its attribute group. The purpose, vision, and mission can be added to this format, if desired. Worksheet 13, is a summary view of the entire architecture.

Brand Promise: We deliver breakthrough products that revolutionize our industry.

Brand Pillar #1: Relevant Innovation

Pillar #1 Narrative: We are adventurous explorers determined to fulfill our need to create, invent, and commercialize revolutionizing technologies, methods, and practices that advance our industry, demonstrates our love and commitment for our customers, and periodically make history.

Behavioral Attributes: Determined, Targeted, Adventurous, Practical

Determined: Narrative here

Targeted: Narrative here

Adventurous: We are fearless innovators who are ready to try new things, to change and evolve with the times, and are open and encouraging of imagination and new paradigms. Our culture balances the current mission needs with a commitment to give each other time to think, explore, express, create, and invent. We invest in learning and tools to support experimentation and development.

Our environment is open, collaborative, and strives to be limitless. We celebrate pushing the boundaries of "what is" regardless if we succeed or fail. Our motto, 'It's better to try and fail then not to have tried at all.

Practical: Narrative here

Operational Attributes:	Disciplined Processes, Invest in People, Open and Loving, Principled Design
Disciplined Processes:	Narrative here (fair, consistent, meaningful, safe, efficient, nimble, agile, and compassionate)
Invest in People:	Narrative here (motivate, challenge, support, coach, reward, diversity, share, and reward)
Open and Loving:	Narrative here (communication, integrity, safety, empathy, compassion, and heart-to-heart)
Principled Design:	Narrative here (brand ambassador, standards, stylish, consistent, organic, user-centric)
Notes:	May include an explanation on how this relates to other pillars or other pillar attributes.

Like part 1, you use your own paper or computer for this worksheet. What follows is a summary structure on a worksheet; where the pillars and attributes are listed in one, two, or three-word summary phrases.

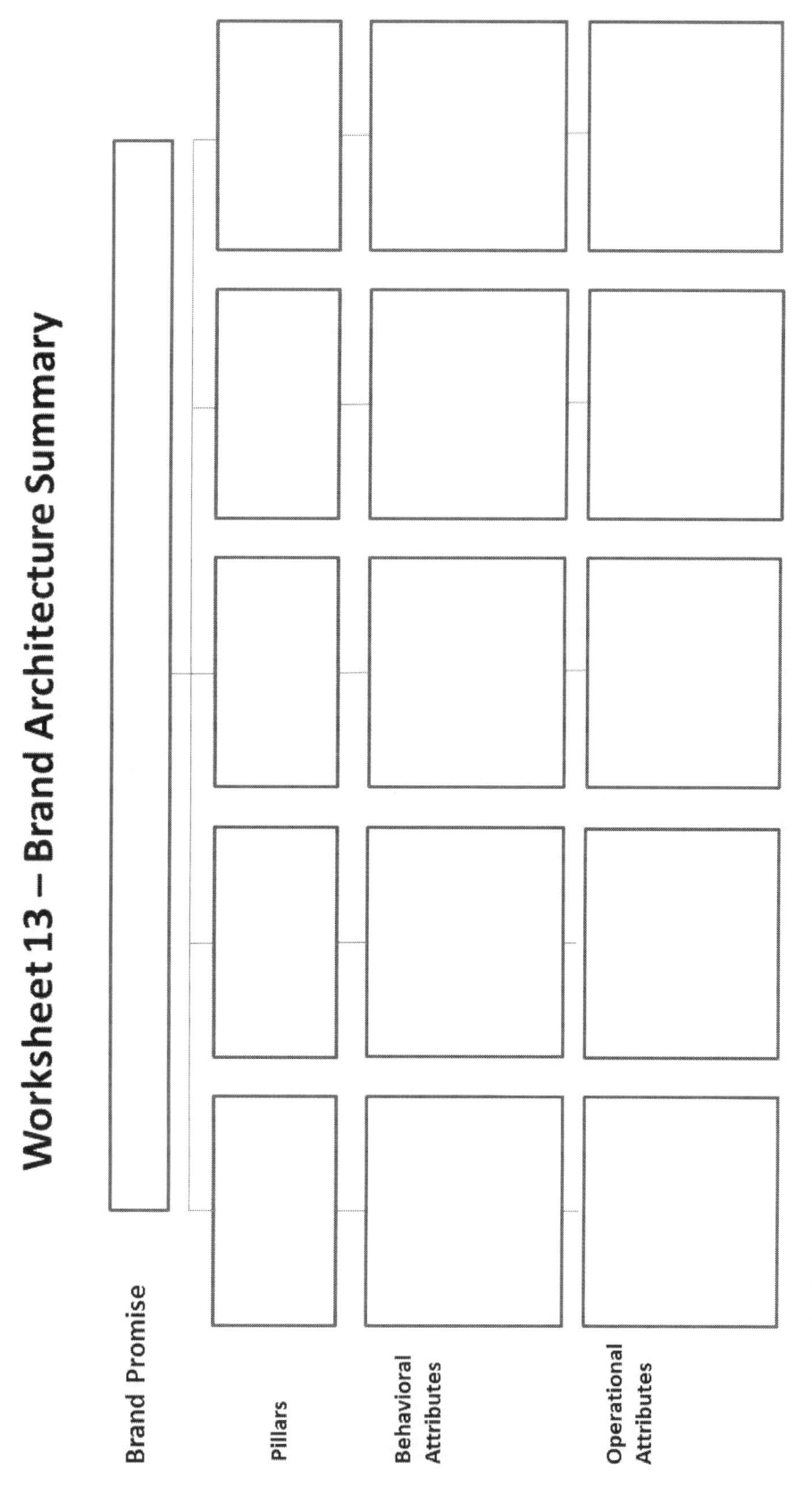

Worksheet 13 – Brand Architecture Summary

Brand Promise

Pillars

Behavioral Attributes

Operational Attributes

Worksheet 14 – Brand Personality

The Brand Personality with the Positioning Statement that follows sets the stage for such things as the firm's product styling, office décor, packaging, and promotional campaigns. It's also the step that leads directly to the development or refresh of the firm's or offering's name and logo. After this activity, Marketing will generally create a brand style guide to ensure the brand is expressed consistently. A style guide is used to inform the expression of the brand across all the senses as well as emotional, physical, and spiritual dimensions. What wine expresses the brand? What color paint evokes the brand within the office?

A Familiar Process

An earlier worksheet used questions like, "If the firm was a hero, who would it be" to tease out some underlying detail and meaning. Below I have returned to these questions and added a few more to help stimulate describing the brand personality outlined by the brand architecture. Remember to explore the positive and negative sides of each answer; the negative sides are the aspects you want to monitor and correct early if they emerge.

- If the firm was a celebrity who would it be?
- What television shows would it watch?
- What kind of car does it drive?
- What mythical creature, being, or item would the firm be?
- What foods does it like?
- What sports does it enjoy playing, if any?
- What animal represents the firm?
- What flavor of ice cream represents the firm?
- A type of décor does the firm like?

Look at the answers and consider what colors, textures, sounds, moods, etc. each one stimulates. See if a pattern emerges. There is some research that shows people respond to sincere, warm, or traditional brands strongly when their elements (color, sound, etc.) are congruent and harmonious. Conversely, the research points out that disruptive or rebel brands resonant stronger with the market when a few elements are dissonant.

After the answers are on the board, I do a vote to determine the top two or three responses to each question. I give everyone two to five votes to cast in each category.

The number of votes provided depends on the length of the list. When completing the form, the teams should think about how the top answers direct the firm's future brand.

Here are two discussion questions that may be helpful:

- Is there a gap between the "as-is," or present personality, and the future "to-be" state?
- How will the gap be addressed?

Worksheet 14 – Brand Personality

1. What emotions or concepts will be linked with the brand?

What positive emotions does the brand enable the consumer to experience? What negative emotions does the firm enable the consumer to eliminate or avoid?

2. Brand Personality

The firm walks into a party and the people turn to see it enter, what are they thinking and feeling when they see it? How is it dressed? How does it carry itself? What image or reputation does it evoke?

Fill in the following blocks based on what will evoke and be associate with the brand.

3. Colors

4. Sounds

5. Texture

6. Shapes

7. Other

Worksheet 14 – Brand Personality

1. What emotions or concepts will be linked with the brand?	2. Brand Personality

Fill in the following blocks based on what will evoke and be associate with the brand.

3. Colors	4. Sounds	5. Texture	6. Shapes	7. Other

Worksheet 15 – Positioning Statement

The Positioning Statement is a key document used to help guide the development of the Integrated Marketing and Communications Plan. It isn't generally used outside of the firm, but it guides the creation of external messages, the elevator speech, and the value proposition. Below is the format I use.

Positioning Statement Structure:

For the customer:	Name of segment
Customers' desire?	What the customer wants to achieve.
Firm's Name:	Name
Unique thing the firm must do to fulfill the customer's desire:	[Name of the key unique differentiator] enables the [name of potential customer segment] to achieve [the desire or outcome and possible measure].
How does the firm specifically do it?	Describe briefly the pivotal way, or ways, the unique thing delivers value. This may also include other differentiators or patents.
Reason to believe the claim:	Compelling evidence that give your potential customer confidence in the firm and its offering – proof points.
Close:	Very short restatement of value to the market

Positioning Statement Example

"For integrated circuit manufactures committed to decreasing their environmental impact, WidgetWiz Inc. provides WaferForge with ResoucSaver technology. WaferForge is the industry's newest high-capacity small footprint refining system for silicon wafer production. The WaferForge has the highest-capacity of any forge in its class, and its patented ResourceSaver protocols save 25% in energy and 10% in water per wafer over previous models. Gains like this are achieved from our patented three-way ultrasound zone refining system and our water management algorithms and feed-forward predictive protocols. Manufactures who are using WaferForge have significantly decreased their environmental impact while increasing production." – 96 words

I work mostly in the B2B world; hence my example is drawn from there. I also use this example as part of an exercise to teach people how to rewrite one loaded with corporate speak and cognitive words to be more emotive, active, and dynamic. Want extra credit? Go ahead and re-write it on your own.

Strategic Positioning Test

The positioning statement, brand architecture, and personality directs the marketing and communications groups in their promotional planning. The statement should contain the firm's or offering's strategic market position and/or unique selling point. In the WidgetWiz example, the firm is positioned primarily as the environmental leader to those customers who hold environment as important.

Start by writing the positioning statement without restriction to length. After completing a draft or two begin to reduce it to no more than 100 words. If the concept is truly known, it can be communicated succinctly.

Next, list the top three competitors to the firm and/or the offering and read the positioning statement with each of their names standing in for the firm's name. Does it read true? If yes, consider reviewing the materials and coming up with a new strategic differentiator or brand position. If the plan was for it to read the same that's okay, if it's a conscious choice. Is the firm then positioning on price? If yes, then lowest cost should be in the statement.

Worksheet 15 – Positioning Statement

Name of target customer segment	
Customer's desire or need	
Firm's name	
Name of key unique differentiator that enables the customer to achieve their aspiration	
Describe briefly the pivotal way or ways the firm delivers value to the customer via the differentiator.	
Proof points – evidence that gives the potential customer confidence in obtaining the promised value.	
Close – short re-statement of value to the market	

Create the Positioning Statement	

Bottoms Up: Doing the Process in Reversing

Generally, I prefer to work in the order the worksheets are shown; however, as mentioned at the beginning of this guide, they can also be worked in reverse. There are two items needed to start in this way. First, the firm needs to pick a set of 5-8 key behavioral attributes it wants to be known for; for example, fun, young, fresh, adventurous, and discerning. Next it needs to create a purpose statement that aligns with these key attributes. The purpose is needed to help set the trajectory. It can be changed at any time, and most likely will be altered as the process goes on. This is one of the items used out of the back-to-front order.

The Positioning Statement is moved up and done after the target segment is selected or even just after the SWOT. The next item is to skip the brand personality section until after the brand promise is completed. Also, it is best to jump over the attribute narratives to list the attributes and their sub-attributes and then go back and do the narratives later. Same process is followed for the pillars. Figure out the pillars first then do the pillar narratives. From here backwards you do things pretty much in order until you get to the SWOT and Environmental Analysis, these are skipped altogether. Okay so maybe it isn't so back-to-front.

For me, I can do this bottom up if I am already very clear on the foundation of the company and where it needs to go.

Wow – Impressive

Time to take a moment, open a favorite beverage, and toast this major milestone. The architecture is done. What's next?

The participants should take at least two-weeks away from this activity. This gives the facilitating team time to pull it all together into a coherent report. Then bring the team back and spend a few hours reviewing it again. Fine tune as needed. Now the real work begins. Planning for implementation. How is the firm going to go from where it is now to where it wants to be? How much time should this program take given the available resources? What are the critical path items that must be funded? Should this be sync'd with the next big product release or started now? How do we train managers to manage for brand? Shameless plug, need a consultant?

Planning and resources are important to making the brand real, but the key item comes down to the management team from top to bottom being committed to this journey over a three-year time frame. Three-years, because it takes time to change the corporate culture, if one already exists, and it takes time for the market to experience the firm and form an opinion. In today's age of social media this can be faster but it's still a multi-year process in many B2B companies. The key is to get the house in order and working before beginning to promote heavily.

What do I mean by committed? It isn't placing posters around the office with cute slogans. It's the management team modeling the behaviors and values, building the processes, and working on creating the brand culture. Many large companies go through the yearly "flavor of the month," embracing this or that with the change of the wind or the yearly change in VPs or CEOs. Under this situation it's difficult for the workforce and the lower level managers to take any new programs seriously. The senior leaders need to be consistent, declare the length of the journey, and stick to it. However, if a situation occurs where change must be made to the plan or brand, the management team needs to be transparent as to why.

Two steps come next. First, create a cross-functional brand team lead by Marketing to run the entire program and act as mentors and evangelists. Ideally, this team should be tied into any customer satisfaction measurement activities and market research being done. Second, management must accept and commit to being trained on how to manage, hire, and model the brand for their teams. If you need any consulting help on this process or implementation feel free to reach out.

Using the Worksheets

Before getting into the dos and don'ts I want to make it clear, I do want people to use the worksheets; however, don't abuse the copyright. These worksheets are available from me in landscape orientation in PowerPoint and PDF. To have these files emailed to you follow the directions at www.okrentconsultingservices.com. The buyer of this book my use the worksheets as much as they wish within their own firm, start-up, or as part of their education about brand or strategic planning.

What will violate my copyright and wishes is incorporating any part of this book into your own "for free" or "for fee" product, service, or presentation. The minimum you must do is include my copyright on every item you use or cite. However, the minimum is because I can't police or enforce anything. Ideally, I would prefer you contact me to discuss paying a small licensing fee for the use of the worksheets or to bulk purchase copies of the DIY book for use with participants. Hey, I want to pay off my house and buy toys too. These rules apply to educational institutions as well. I don't consider making copies of the worksheets in bulk as student handouts part of "Fair Use." I consider it unfair abuse.

I leave it to your own honor and integrity to police this request.

Contact Information

Feel free to email your questions and/or feedback.

David A. Okrent
Okrent Consulting Services
Telephone: + 1 206 390-3806
Email: info@okrentconsultingservices.com
www.okrentconsultingservices.com
www.heartcentricmarketing.com

Check out Okrent Consulting Services on Facebook.

Printed in Great Britain
by Amazon